RHODA BAXTER AND JANE
LOVERING

How to Write Romantic Comedy

First published by Juxtaposition Publishing 2019

First edition

ISBN: 978-1-913752-00-2

*This book was professionally typeset on Reedsy.
Find out more at reedsy.com*

Contents

I

How to write romantic comedy - the comedy part

This is your introduction in how to write funny prose.

1

What's so funny about love?

Laughter is a great thing – it lifts your mood, burns calories, helps reduce pain [1]and reduces your blood pressure in the long run. And everyone loves a good love story. So if you can combine the two, you've got to be onto a winner... right?

Romantic comedy (or rom com) is a hugely popular genre. At its very basic level, it's a romance, with funny bits. It's easier if you think about films rather than books because the mish-mash of marketing terms that have been used for romance novels with comedy in have muddied the waters somewhat. You have a girl or a boy (or a non-binary person) who meets a boy or a girl (or a non-binary person), they are usually in some sort of conflict, they flirt a bit, they realise they're falling in love, they may even get together, then things go horribly wrong, they overcome whatever it was that was holding them back and finally, *finally*, they get a happy ending.

For it to be a romance, you must have a happy ending. It doesn't have to be 'Happy Ever After', 'Happy For Now' will do. If you don't have a happy ending, my friend, you have not written a romance.

For it to be a comedy, it has to be funny. That's where this book comes in.

Different types of romantic comedy

We're going to call it rom com from now on, because, frankly, who has the time for 'antic' and 'edy'. They don't even rhyme. We'll leave them here to amuse themselves for a while.

Where were we... oh yes. Here are few examples of rom coms. This list is here to give you an idea of the breadth of the genre.

TL;DR - If it's got romance and comedy in it... you can probably call it a rom com.

Bridget Jones' Diary by Helen Fielding- the book that sparked the flame of chicklit. It's an epistolary retelling of *Pride and Prejudice*, written in the form of a diary. It hit the zeitgeist of the early 90s and millions of young women identified with the main character.

The Secret Dream World of a Shopaholic by Sophie Kinsella - the successor to Bridget Jones. A story about a compulsive shopper who somehow ends up writing a financial advice column. This is the book that embodied the ditsy, accident prone, designer shoe obsessed heroine that became synonymous with chicklit. Unusually for a chicklit heroine, Becky Bloomberg (the Shopaholic) went on to star in a whole series of books.

Living Dangerously - the first book by Katie Fforde, who went on to be one of the best known romance writers in the UK. Katie's books have lovely Cotswold settings and have a very comforting air about them, even when they tackle serious subjects. These are probably veering closer to light (as in 'not dark') women's fiction.

Afternoon Tea at the Sunflower Cafe by Milly Johnson - This is Rhoda's favourite by this author - who is another star of the UK rom com charts. Her books are regional romantic comedies. The books are heart-warming and funny and excellent reads wherever you're from, but if you know the region (Yorkshire) they are even funnier because you recognise the quirks that people have.

I don't Know How She Does It by Allison Pearson - a very popular book book about a woman juggling marriage, career and motherhood. The first book to become popular which had a heroine who was older (in her thirties - gasp!). It is also more about keeping love alive than falling in love itself, so it's technically not a rom com, but gets classed as one anyway. It hit the zeitgeist in the late 90s/early 2000s and millions of young mums identified with it (possibly the same ones who identified with Bridget Jones when they were younger...).

To All The Boys I've Loved Before by Jenny Han - trope driven YA rom com. Notable in that it is a book about a half Korean heroine, written by a Korean author. It's so much fun. Also notable because it got turned into a film by Netflix and everyone was talking about it for a while.

Shaun of the Dead - okay, not a book. It's a film. It's mentioned here because it's a zom rom com and you don't get many of those.

Rachel's Holiday by Marian Keyes - this is one of those books that modern rom com authors cite as 'the book that made me want to write'. It's about addiction and is dark and deeply moving, but also has jokes in it. This is what Jane and Rhoda both like to write. :-)

[1] Dunbar, R. I. M.; Baron, R.; Frangou, A.; Pearce, E.; van Leeuwen, E. J. C.; Stow, J.; Partridge, G.; MacDonald, I.; Barra, V.; van Vugt, M. (2011). "Social laughter is correlated with an elevated pain threshold". Proceedings of the Royal Society B: Biological Sciences. 279 (1731): 1161–1167

2

The Comic Premise

Laughter is the way we react to a joke. It's a very old response, wired deep into our animal brains. No matter what language we speak, we all laugh. [1] It's a social signal to say 'I'm all right', it's a way to show we belong to part of a group, it's an exercise in power, it's all of these things and more.

Laughing is a social activity. We laugh more, louder when we're with other people. Sometimes, if someone's giggle is contagious enough, we will all laugh when there's no joke at all. But reading is a solitary activity. As writers, we can't really replicate the social side of things, but we can use humour to produce laughter. If we're really lucky, we get readers complaining that they laughed out loud on the bus and got funny looks.

One popular theory is that laughter is a modified fear response. When we perceive a threat, our body responds, putting us into a heightened state of tension. If that threat is suddenly removed, the drop in tension released a burst of endorphins, and we laugh.

When we tell a joke, we are trying to replicate this in the mind of the reader (or listener).

Every joke has at least two components - the set up and the punchline. The set-up is where the joker (not The Joker, he's creepy, I mean the person telling a joke; that joker) builds the scenario, leading you towards one conclusion. Tension mounts up in your mind and body as you anticipate where the story is going to go and predict ending to the story. You lean in. And then … BAM! The punchline subverts the expected ending. It switches track and takes the story an entirely different direction. There is a split second where your brain analyses the information you've just had and realises that it still applies to the new situation introduced by the punchline. The difference between what you expect and what you get makes you laugh. Pleasure centres are stimulated and you get that lovely little endorphin hit. A little like you've escaped from danger.

Generally speaking, the higher the tension before the punchline, the bigger the 'relief' and the bigger the laugh.

This would be why people working in stressful situations - medics, rescue workers and the like - use jokes, often with very dark humour, to alleviate the tension. It's a pressure release valve.

As writers we can use this to puncture the tension in a scene - either because the characters needed it, or because you want to release a tiny bit of pressure so that you can build it up again in the next scene.

So how do you create this gap between what is expected and what is delivered?

There are lots of ways to describe it - the comic premise, the expectation gap, the incongruity gap - but we like to call it Juxtaposition of Thingies. We came up with that after careful thought, obviously … not because we both had a moment of brain fog and couldn't remember actual words. Nope. Not at all.

Humour comes from the gap between what you expect and what actually happens. Generally speaking, the bigger the gap, the funnier it is. But if the gap is too big, people may not make the jump.

So how to do you create the gap? Easy. Juxtapose things.

How to juxtapose your thingies

1. Mismatched characters - juxtapose personalities

This is the basis of every odd couple scenario you've ever seen, including the brilliantly titled *The Odd Couple*.

The difference between how the different characters react to the same situation, leads to all kinds of amusing scenarios. Ideally you need at least one character that the audience can identify with. It doesn't have to be the same character right the way through, but each scene needs one character who represents the 'normal' interpretation.

You can have an odd character in a normal world - *Mork and Mindy* is a great example of this. Mork is an alien and doesn't respond to anything in the way you'd expect. Similarly, *Mr Bean* is funny because whatever he does, it's not what you'd expect a normal person to do in that situation. Mr Bean's situations are in themselves a little odd and generally the scenarios are simple and easy to understand, which makes the show appealing to young children and adults alike. *Johnny English*, on the other hand, is even funnier because the gap isn't just between what you'd expect him to do and what he actually does... but also between how he sees himself and how he actually is (see Dramatic Irony in the next chapter).

Another option is to have one sane character in an odd world. Penny in the early series of *The Big Bang Theory* is a normal person surrounded by oddball geniuses. Tim in the UK version of *The Office* is another 'normal' person who has to deal with working in a team of odd personalities. Penny and Tim's reactions to what is going on around them represents the viewer and what they would expect and provides a built-in contrast to the wackiness of the other characters.

Do you really need to have a 'normal' person in the show? Not necessarily. A group of extreme or unusual characters can be hilarious - like *Red Dwarf* or *The IT Crowd*. But in each of these, in any given situation, one of the characters will advocate the 'normal' solution. They pass the baton between them, creating the feeling of an ensemble of oddballs.

Probably the most useful method of creating the expectation gap when it comes to writing the rom com is to have a few instances of someone doing something weird in response to an otherwise normal situation. For example, Sophie Kinsella's *How to Be an Undomestic Goddess* begins with the heroine trying to get a job as a housekeeper simply because she refuses to believe she might NOT get the job. Once she gets offered the job, her stubbornness means she has to keep going to 'prove' she can do it. This fierce competitive streak is entirely in keeping with the character. She doesn't step outside her normal self to do something weird. It's all properly foreshadowed, so that when we see her do something strange, while we cover our eyes and say 'noooo', we also understand why she did it.

2. Comic characters - Juxtapose worldviews

A comic character (or even a group of them) has a unique view of the world which governs how they behave. Eg. *Father Ted*, *Blackadder*, *Toast of London*, *The Big Bang Theory*. [If you haven't seen any of these comedies (let's skip over the bit where we stare at you with faintly horrified expressions) we suggest you rush off and do so as soon as you finish reading this book, and making notes. You are making notes, right?]

In romance we don't often use comic characters as heroines (with the honorable exception of Becky Bloomberg in the shopaholic series) because we need them to be relatable. There was a time when the clumsy heroine was popular, but now they're likely to be branded too stupid to live and taken outside and shot ... or the reader just gives up in annoyance, which amounts to the same thing (what do you mean 'not really'?)

But there's no reason you can't use them as secondary characters. The wacky best friend is an often used trope. As we've said before though, be careful not to make them two dimensional. They need to be real people, even if they have odd ideas about what's normal.

Similarly, you can create humour in the gap between what a character says and what they actually do. Becky Bloomberg is a good example (again! It has all the good stuff, does Shopaholic).

3. Fish out of water - Juxtapose situations against character reactions

This is another common trope - the big city lawyer goes to work as a housekeeper (*How to be an Undomestic Goddess*), city girl inherits a share in a auctioneering house (Katie Fforde's *Flora's Lot*) just about anyone opens a cup cake shop. The difference between how the heroine's expectations and how things are actually done in the new place are full of comedic potential.

Probably the most useful method of creating a comic situation when it comes to writing the rom com is to have a few instances of someone doing something weird in response to an otherwise normal situation. This provides the way to set up the situation. Then make things worse - but always, always, make sure the characters are true to themselves.

This is closely related to the comic characters. You can surround your 'normal' heroine with outlandish characters. Better still, put them into conflict with other normal people and see if you can pull comedy out of that.

4. Absurd Humour - Juxtapose... well... anything

There is a time and place for absurdity and to be honest, a rom com is probably the wrong place for it. You can have the odd spark of absurdity, maybe in someone's reaction to something, or in dialogue, but really, it's hard to sustain it over the course of whole book. That's why a lot of absurd humour is sketch based. You can't stretch it out without adding other comedic elements.

Monty Python's Flying Circus was great at absurd humour. The associated films combined satire with elements of the absurd to great effect. Similarly, *The Mighty Boosh*, which combined brilliant comic characters and hints of the absurd with traditional sit-com storylines. I'm trying to think of an American example... er... *Pee Wee Herman*, perhaps.

5. Dramatic irony - Juxtapose what the character knows against what they think they know

This is where the audience know more than the characters. This is a great device for creating tension (because the reader knows that the person the heroine is about to fall for is a baddie – but the heroine doesn't!). You can also use it for comedy. *The Back to the Future* movies (and a lot of time travel stories) use dramatic irony for comedy because the main character and the audience know what the future holds, whilst the rest of the characters in the past don't. So when Marty tells Doc that the president in his time in the future is Ronald Reagan (at that point in the past, he was just an actor), Doc finds it funny. The audience finds it funnier because it's actually true.

You can have dramatic irony in the gap between how the character predicts things are going to be and how they actually end up (for example, Bridget Jones predicts that she'll look sophisticated and smooth on her weekend away in the posh hotel, but in reality, she ends up wind blown and missing half the things she needs).

You can also make the gap through the difference between how the character sees themselves and how they appear to the reader. For example Basil Fawlty (in *Fawlty Towers*), Johnny English, Bertie Wooster and oh, so many more. If you want an old school example, Mr Pickwick of *The Pickwick Papers*.

In real life, this is why we find a lot of things kids say to be cute and funny. Things they believe to be true are, sadly, not really true. As adults we know this and find it funny. It's a pity really. Some of the stuff they believe is fantastic. Except, maybe, the dragons.

6. Schadenfreude - not really a juxtaposition

This is where you see something terrible happen to someone else and you laugh because you're so relieved that it's not you. It relies on the reader laughing *at* a character rather than laughing *with* them. Once you get beyond the slipping on banana skins or falling face first into a cake type gags, it borders on being cruel. Use sparingly. If at all.

All this boils down to juxtaposing one thing against another. When we first gave this talk, Jane presented wearing a penguin onesie. Now, there's nothing funny about a onesie. Or about J-... er ... a woman giving a presentation. But someone standing in front of a room giving a serious presentation, whilst dressed as a penguin. That's funny because it's unexpected.

So get your thingies. Juxtapose them in unexpected ways and *et voila* - the funny.

[1] Gervais, Matthew; Sloan Wilson, David (2005). "The Evolution and Functions of Laughter and Humor: A Synthetic Approach". *Quarterly Review of Biology*. **80** (4): 395–430.

3

The different types of comedy

We've decided (or maybe the powers that be have decided, we can't remember), that there are seven different types of comedy. Some of them work better in a written format than others (just try writing down someone slipping on a banana skin – it's not funny at all as a series of words. There are those who would argue it's not funny as a visual gag either, but those people usually are usually in charge of Health and Safety, and will point out that nobody should be eating in the workplace and her shoes are unsuitable for heavy lifting, so we can disregard them).

Anyway. On to the types of comedy that we have decided on. And do bear in mind that most of these subsections of comedy have a huge amount of cross-over between them.

1. Observational Comedy

Observational comedy is generally that of the 'quiet wit' rather than the hysterical laughter, but it works well in written form. It's the throwaway line when your couple meet and she describes his hair as being like a Brillo pad that two dogs have had a fight over. It's best described as a new way of looking at an old scene, a new way of putting something every day into words. It's the humour of the really good stand-up comedian who can riff on the subject of, say, conversations on the bus, or the ridiculousness of clouds for an hour. The fact that you can listen to (or read) it and have a reaction of "gosh, I never thought of it like that, but – yes!" is what makes it funny.

Good observational comedy has the interplay between humour and truth. It makes the everyday different (which is kind of what writing is all about, when you think about it) and it's usually the sheer unexpectedness that makes your reader laugh. Or smile. We'll settle for smiling.

2. Character Based Comedy

This can either take the form of characters who are intrinsically amusing because of who they are, their role in life or their appearance (ditzy type sidekick who always wears high heels however unsuitable they are for what she is doing, because she thinks they make her look taller) or because they are prone to saying amusing things. Again, the humour in the unexpected comes here. Try not to create characters simply in order for them to be 'the funny one', this can lead to horrible examples of stereotyping, think, for example of that often overused trope of "gay best friend". Even your 'funny' characters should have a believable role in your novel and not simply stagger on to be funny and then vanish only to reappear when you need them to come and be funny again.

Our favourite comic examples come from the interaction of characters in comic situations (we'll get to that bit later). Character based comedy works well in partnership with observational comedy, the way a particular person looks at the world and verbalises it is the starting point of most novels, after all.

3. Dark Comedy

Some of the funniest people I have ever known have been those who work in the professions that cause them to see some of the most awful things. Nurses and firemen spring to mind (and not just because I like the uniforms). They joke about death, disfigurement and injuries – things that you wouldn't think could be funny (but, as you will find as you write more comedy, there is *nothing* that can't be funny). They joke to relieve tension, they joke to bring light into really tragic situations, and also because the human brain can only bear so much awfulness before a coping mechanism cuts in, which is often humour. In a dark place, people will laugh. The humour tends to be subtle of course, nobody is ever going to fall about laughing about the fact that their leg is hanging off, but human nature dictates that, wherever there is some big awfulness going on, there is someone else making a joke about it. Also bear in mind that, if you are writing a big tragic scene, a little lightness can make that dark seem even darker.

4. Situational Comedy

Situation Comedy, or Sit Com, is the name given to those comedies on TV, where a lot of the laughter comes from the viewers' familiarity with the setting, which remains the same from week to week. The comedy comes partly from them being in a particular location that is integral to everything they do. Now, that can be a space station (where you can, apparently, get quite a lot of giggle-mileage from something as simple as two people in space suits running out of air) or a hairdresser's, or two people sharing a flat.

In books, situational comedy is very similar. However, it is your characters that your reader will be identifying with and laughing (hopefully) with, so the situation is usually funny because of the people you put into it. Here we have scenarios like the city couple who are forced to go and live in the countryside. The countryside is not, intrinsically, amusing. I know this, I live in it. It's generally just like everywhere else only with more smells and fewer shops. However, when you people it with those who have no idea what silage is, it becomes funny (at least, it does to all of us who do know what silage is).

Situational comedy can also be transient. You can have one scene where the set-up leads to the comedy, just take the 'meeting the parents' scenario. It's not humour based on the location in this case, but on the fact that this is a situation that most people can relate to. 'Going shopping' is a situation, as is 'finding a dead body'. Although we'd hope that most people can't relate to that last one, they can still imagine themselves in that situation. Again, although the situation may or may not be amusing in itself, it is your characters that will give rise to the humour, because of the way that they interact, both with each other and with the situation in question. Often a comic character will react to a normal situation in an unexpected (even bizarre) way that is entirely in keeping with their character. For examples, see *Father Ted*.

5. Physical Comedy

Now, this is one of the hardest to get over in written format. Pratfalls, spilled tea, and sudden unexpected coughing fits can all be very funny in real life, but once you take them to pieces to describe them for your reader, they lose a lot of the humour. It's a bit like a car. Seeing a beautiful Audi (other manufacturers are available) is one thing. Watching it stripped to its component parts is quite another. You lose the view of the overall object and its working parts are visible, which is often what happen when writing physical comedy. You know that thing with two men and a plank? When one is swinging round and catching the other man with the end, and sometime he ducks and the plank does something unexpected? It's very hard to describe that in words and still make it funny.

So much of humour is planting a small idea in the mind of the reader, and then they do the heavy lifting work of laughing. If you successfully put that tiny idea in – say with a brief description of your scenario – then their minds will go to work on the detail, and they will, almost, make their own humour.

Physically, falling in a cow pat is uncomfortable, and sometimes painful. However, if you describe a field of cow pats, put your character in there and then mention that they are crossing that field, you don't have to over describe what is happening to them, a simple 'ow!' or 'whooooooaaaahhhh!' will be enough, because your reader will be putting the actions in for themselves. So, yes, physical comedy can be an element in your novel, but be careful how you handle it, or it might blow up in your face (with hilarious consequences, naturally).

6. Pun Based Comedy

Puns can be very, very funny. But they are like salt in cooking. They add a certain something to your writing, but only if used sparingly. Overdone, they can make your reader sick. They do work well in the written format, but beware using a pun that is based on pronunciation, 'It's National Book Day, why are you making a clown outfit?' 'I just thought I'd make the jester' (gesture ... see my books for other feeble examples). When it's said, it's funnier than it is written down and although your reader is reading it, *your characters are saying it*.

Conversely, beware of the pun used in conversation that is only funny when the words are seen (any bridle/bridal gags). If you say it, it's not funny, but your characters are using it in conversation. It's things like this that can pull your reader out of the book. You never want them to remember that what they are doing is reading a book – you want them to remain so immersed in your world that they feel they are part of the action. And when someone says 'do you want a bit for that bridle outfit?' and everyone falls about because it's so funny, your reader may just roll their eyes.

There's also the risk that the reader may not 'get' the pun. While a pun is difficult to unsee once you've seen it, sometimes it can take a while to work it out. You don't want the reader to pause and think about what they just read because, as we mentioned before, we don't want them to remember that they're reading a book. So puns. Use sparingly.

7. Gross Out Comedy

Now, I've never found gross humour funny, but I am aware that I am not truly representative of the human race, so feel obligated to cover it here. Whether it is actually 'funny' or whether due to the human tendency to laugh in the face of shock, is debatable, but it exists, so, here we are. Gross out humour is more often deployed in books (and films) aimed at younger readers, the late teens and early twenties. By later life we've often grown out of the ability to find humour in others' misfortunes, although there is still a tiny pleasure in Schadenfreude, and watching a villain get their comeuppance in a particularly unpleasant way can find a receptive audience.

The line between dark humour and gross out humour can be a fine one to tread; both often rely on the shock value to create laughter, but whereas dark humour can be employed in romantic comedies, gross out humour doesn't cross into our kind of fiction quite as readily. If you are a huge fan of *American Pie* films you may beg to differ, of course. Anyway. Gross out humour relies on a suspension of subtlety as well as disbelief, and can be funny if used sparingly.

Since gross out comedy is about breaking a taboo, we should probably mention swearing. Sometimes swearing is ****** funny. But there are people who are offended by words like ******* or *&$*! Or even, ££££$£ (gasp!). You know your readers better than we do. Use your judgement with the swearing.

8. Parody

You don't see parody very much in rom com. The main problem with writing a parody is that you don't know whether the reader knows about the original thing that you're parodying. People who've seen/read the original might find the book hilarious, but those who haven't would be left mildly bemused. If you really want to parody something, make sure it's so well known that everyone will get what you're trying to do. In rom com you might be able to get away with a scene or two of parody, but it would be difficult to sustain over a whole book.

4

Uses of Comedy

Why bother with comedy in your novels? Would a good joke make your searing novel about ambition and hubris more memorable ... well, it might do. It's all very well putting jokes into a narrative, but it's even better to realise that they're there for a purpose.

1. Use humour to reveal character

Humour is subjective. A joke that makes you laugh like a drain may not even raise a smile from someone else. What you find funny depends on who you are and what moulded your sense of humour. The same is true for your characters. You can use this in your writing, by asking why.

If you have a joker, one who always has to make a joke... you have to wonder why. Are they using humour to deflect attention from themselves? To make themselves easier to like? It's no accident that a lot of comedians say they were bullied when they were young. Perhaps they used humour to deflect attention from their vulnerabilities. This basic self defence mechanism, learned as a child as a way to avoid being bullied, would stay with them into adulthood. Me, I'm very short and chubby. At school, I knew someone would make a dig about my height, so I used to get a height joke in before they did. Generally, it meant that people didn't bother making any more comments about my height and we could get on with more normal conversation instead.

They could be using humour to distract themselves from painful thoughts. Humour and pain are related. Laughter is known to reduce physical pain. When they said laughter was the best medicine, they weren't joking (See what I did there?). That character who is incapable of being serious may be doing that so that they don't have to feel the inevitable pain that being serious would bring. As with all things - think about how you can use this in the story.

Some people make jokes when they're nervous. Why is your character nervous? Are they cracking more jokes than usual? Are they distracting themselves or others by making people laugh? Why?

Perhaps they don't want to reveal something. Making a joke can be a good way to stop having to talk about something. If this is the case - what is it they don't want to talk about? What can you do to force them to talk about it? How does the hiding (or revelation) of the secret affect the other characters?

Do they have a particularly unusual sense of humour? One laced with a hint of cruelty, perhaps? Or humour that displays a lack of real empathy? The things people joke about and how they react when someone doesn't laugh at their jokes can reveal a lot about a character.

2. Use humour to gain reader sympathy

Giving a character a sense of humour can be a great way to make a character 'sympathetic'. Who doesn't like someone who makes them laugh?

The object is to get the reader to be on the side of the character. Throw a difficult situation at them (the character, not the reader) and have them resolve it with good sense and good humour. The reader will always end up on their side by the end of the event. This is how we end up on the side of the lovable rogue - like Flynn Rider (*Tangled*) or Jack Sparrow (*Pirates of the Caribbean*).

In old style romcoms, heroines were given character traits like clumsiness, or not being able to stop talking, even when they were digging themselves deeper and deeper into a hole - the idea was that the reader would feel that character's embarrassment and cringe on their behalf, and from then on, they're on the protagonist's side. Done well, this works. Done less well, it's annoying and makes the heroine look like a fool. Readers even have a term for it 'Too Stupid To Live'. You don't have to be as obvious as this.

3. To contrast with darker scenes

You can use funny scenes next to darker ones to accentuate the dark scene and make it more poignant. In the same way that a white object stands out against a black background, the contrast between the humour in the scene before will make a sad scene feel much sadder. If you've been smiling along, reading the story and you hit a sad scene (which has been foreshadowed), you will feel it more keenly. Try it.

In a darker book, a bit of humour can give the reader a little breathing space and stop the book from becoming unrelentingly bleak.

Similarly, a joke in a sad situation, can make the whole scene feel more poignant.

4. To make unpleasant statements palatable

'There's many a true word spoken in jest' - proverb

The best comedy has a basis in truth, or even pain. Humour is often used to soften the blow when making an unpleasant point. For example, there's the now famous sketch where Donald Glover makes the point about domestic abuse: 'Everyone has a crazy ex-girlfriend story. Why are there no crazy ex-boyfriend stories? Because if you have a crazy boyfriend, you gonna die'.

There are truths that people find difficult to hear and wrapping it up with humour can get it past their defences and make them think about it.

Be careful not to take things too far though. You don't want to stray into the territory of bad taste with your home truths. Some statements will never be palatable. See Ricky Gervais for examples that skirt the line between acceptable and not.

5. To see the familiar in a different light

Humour is often the by-product of seeing the world from a different angle. Satire relies on this. But you can use humour to make your reader see something in a different light. Or make a joke where the punchline actually makes you think about something you'd taken for granted. How many times have you heard a comment on a satirical program that first made you laugh... and then made you think?

Pretty much all topical satire does this. If you need a current example, see the latest episode of *Have I Got News For You*. Or if you're in the US, *Saturday Night Live* or *The Daily Show*.

6. To make things more memorable

People remember jokes far better than they remember facts. This is a fact.[1]

A good joke can make a scene memorable. Or you can use a joke to draw attention to something you want the reader to remember later.

I bet you've learned more about politics by watching political satire than by reading newspapers. I know I have.

7. To have fun

We all know that writing a book is hard work. It's fun for about 5000 words and then it's a just a slog to get the first draft done. Since you're spending 70 to 80 thousand words with these characters, you may as well have fun with them. If you enjoy what you're writing, you'll feel better and it will show in your writing. With mentoring newbie writers, I've read books where, even if the plot was a little bit loose and the book wasn't quite ready, the sheer joy of a writer having fun shone through. Fixing a plot is easy. Injecting a sense of fun into writing when it isn't there already is hard. Not impossible. But hard.

[1] Carlson, *Humor - International Journal of Humor Research* 24(1) · February 2011

5

Different types of jokes

No, this doesn't mean funny and unfunny. There really are different ways of 'structuring' your humour to give it more impact or, in other words, to make it funnier. Warning – this section may contain examples …

1. The Rule of Three

Less of a rule, more a sort of guideline, to quote *Pirates of the Caribbean*, things are funnier in threes. The first example sets up the scene, the second reiterates the normality, and the third confounds expectation, to put in in a more scholarly fashion. Think of all those 'an Englishman, a Scotsman and an Irishman go into a bar' jokes, that's rule of three. The Englishman sets up the joke, the Scotsman continues the pattern, giving rise to the expectation of what comes next, and then the Irishman turns it all around – and that's what makes the laugh.

So three is the minimum number of examples you need in

order to complete the joke. Two examples doesn't give the opportunity for the normality of the situation to be properly established and, again to quote, Monty Python this time, four is right out.

Here's another example of the rule of three, this time in dialogue:

"What shall we watch tonight? *Newsnight* are doing a searing indictment of poverty in the clothing industry, or there's that documentary on the effects of fracking on the wildlife of New Zealand. Or there's *Strictly*."

Your first two program choices set up the character as an intellectual who likes to watch documentaries which go in depth into current events. The third reveals the reality, that they actually like lowbrow popular entertainment, but rank them on a par with the more esoteric programming. Having been led to believe that your character is this deep thinking academic, the final example turns your expectation on its head and reveals them to be just as prone to celebrities in twirly frocks as everyone else. And it's this surprise, this juxtaposition of ideas (or 'thingies') that makes your reader laugh.

There is something about the rhythm of 'three' that is pleasing to the ear – think about all the fairy tales where there are three bears, three billy goats or three little pigs. Or this example, where there are three elements. If I'd written 'three bears, three billy goats, three little pigs and three musketeers', your eyes would have got bored somewhere around the goats, just seeing the sentence running on and on. By the time I'd got to pigs, you would have wandered off to see if there were any biscuits in the cupboard. And then you would never have got the three musketeers, and that would, quite frankly, have served you right.

Can I put in a link to my favourite scene from *The Life of Brian* in here? Please. It's a great example of the rule of three:

Brian tells his followers they are all individuals.

The followers repeat in unison "Yes, we are all individuals."

Brian tells them they are all different.

The followers, again in unison, chant, "Yes, we are all different."

Pause.

One person in the crowd says, "Er... I'm not."

Person next to them says, "shhh."

This works on several levels. You've got the rule of three. You've got dramatic irony in that what the crowd is saying is directly at odds with what they're doing. You've got a lovely pause between the set up and the punchline and then, you have a topper (a joke that builds on the punchline) with the second person saying 'shhh'. It's damn near perfect.

2. Reactions and Reflections

Now this, for me, comes under 'observational humour'. It's a bit like *'l'espirit de l'escalier'* – which is the proper name for the state of waking up at three in the morning with the *perfect reply* to that thing your colleague said at four o'clock in the afternoon. The perfect witty riposte, just that little bit too late. When you are writing romantic comedies you can put that perfect reply in *at the perfect time*. And none of your readers will know that you had to go away for three days and sit staring at a wall in order to come up with that 'off the cuff' remark, because your characters will come up with it at exactly the right time. That's the 'reactions' part of this section. The perfect witty statement, the puncturing of bombast, it can be placed just right to make your reader laugh, probably because they wish that it was the sort of thing that *they* would come up with in that situation.

Reflection is similar, but more internalised. It is the witty turn of phrase that you monologue to yourself or observe to a listener. Again, we are trying to describe the everyday in a new, original and hopefully surprising way and it is that surprise, that confounding of the expectation of normality which will make the reader laugh.

So you could have your character thinking about a potential boyfriend as 'he's all right. Well, he's upright and employed and that's two up on my last bloke'. And it's funny because we'd normally think of being employed as a desirable trait in a potential partner, but being upright as absolutely essential, and the thought of a previous man being neither of these things creates an amusing mental image of our character trying to interact with someone permanently supine. Or a character thinking about her best friend's new, much younger boyfriend. 'I don't know what she's thinking. I've got shoes in my wardrobe older than him. Hell, I've got *bread* older than him.'

You can also have funny reactions from the other characters. Depending on how you've set up the relationship between the protagonist and their friends, you could potentially have some very funny reactions to what they say and do. This is another good reason to have a best friend character, they can provide comedy with your protagonist playing the straight man (or woman).

3. Running Gags

Running gags are jokes or phrases that, fairly predictably, run throughout the entire book. Think of Sheldon in *The Big Bang Theory* and his 'knock knock knock, Penny' (Rule of Three again, see?). It can be repeated in various settings and under various conditions and the familiarity is what makes the audience laugh. We know what's coming, we know how this joke works and it helps to make us feel part of the action, part of the gang. *The Fast Show*, if you remember it (it had Mr Weasley in it), was based almost entirely on running gags.

You can thread similar jokes through your writing. A description, a saying, an observation or even a quote from somewhere else can be repeated, woven through the action to give the reader a jolt of the familiar. They *know* the punchline, they are waiting for it, the waiting builds the tension and the delivery gives a nice satisfying hit of dopamine. It's from that 'aah' of recognition that the humour is derived. We've all picked up sayings, memes and statements that we use to reinforce our tribe (try saying 'Live long and prosper' at a WI meeting for an illustration of how your tribe needs to be on a similar wavelength for this to work), and a similar mechanism exists in fiction. When repeated jokes crop up, your reader feels included. Part of the 'tribe' which contains your characters. This is what makes a running joke successful.

However, we do have to put in a caveat here. Be. Careful. Running gags only work under two specific circumstances –

Firstly, that it's not repeated so often that your reader thinks it's just been put in for comic effect and gets tired of anticipating the punchline. Readers can feel that you are cheating a little by deriving repeat laughs from something previously set up to be funny, and it can get, dare I say, a bit *boring*. Take Sheldon and his knocking. Once an episode is fine and funny. Twice, and we still laugh, especially if the circumstances are different. Three times (and this is where Rule of Three doesn't always hold true) and we've seen it, we've laughed at it twice and the humour is beginning to pall. Any more and we are wondering whether the script writers were on holiday that week. The only exception is if, at the third repetition something different happens. Then the first two repetitions were just the set up for that last one… which is all getting a bit meta.

Secondly, your gag has to be understood. Imagine, if you will, a cartoon character whose catchphrase is 'An apple a day is too much for a dog!' I know and love this cartoon and, whilst writing a book, I conceive a running gag where characters say 'an apple a day is too much for a dog!' to one another. Of course, anyone who also knows and loves the cartoon character I am referring to will get the joke and find it funny. Anyone who has never seen or heard of the cartoon in question might find it oddly amusing the first time. Maybe the second time. By the third time I use the gag, they are going to wonder if I have lost my marbles and am just writing random words. So, know your tribe. (If you've never seen *The Big Bang Theory*, you are going to feel this way about my Sheldon example. Sorry).

An honourable mention is due here for the call-back joke. This is a joke that refers back to an earlier joke, usually at the end of the scene, or sometimes at the end of the story. This is often a good way to end a book with the required aww factor without making your characters drown in cheesy lines. Apart from giving the reader a warm and fuzzy feeling of inclusion, recalling something that was said somewhere at the start of the characters' relationship gives the story a pleasing sense of completion, as though you've closed a circle. It doesn't work for all stories, obviously, but if you're really stuck for an ending, have a look and see if you can use a joke, ideally just the punchline, from earlier in the story to end with a laugh.

4. Suspension of Disbelief

You can get away with anything in fiction. Seriously. I've written about vampires and people with quite lowly jobs who can afford to live in lovely houses, and both of these things require a degree of suspension of disbelief on the part of the reader. The main thing to be wary of is that you set your rules at the start. This applies to *all* fiction, it's not specific to comedy, or even to romantic comedy, but you might find that your comedy loses its edge a little if your rules aren't consistent.

Let's take a situation that we've mentioned previously. The city couple moving to the country and protesting about the smell of silage and the noise of cows. You've set this situation up, your readers are finding the 'fish out of water' scenario funny, all well and good. But you have to keep it consistent. You can't suddenly reveal that one of your characters was born in rural Wales and knows how to milk a cow, however much that might set up your romance with the gorgeous farmer next door. If your character was born in the country, they will know all about silage, even if they have lived in the city for twenty years. You lose that element that was making things funny, that scenario that your reader was invested in.

Another situation. Your ditzy protagonist has spent all her

rent money on having her hair done, and can't afford to pay. But, fear not! Her landlord will let her work off the rent if she milks the cows that he inexplicably now keeps in the garden because this is a scenario I really didn't think through before I started writing it. This is only funny if you've set up the scene whereby this has either happened before, or there is an arrangement between Ditzy Protagonist and Landlord that she can do this. Otherwise your reader is seeing a bonkers woman who spends money on hairdressing and may well be out on the street by evening. Although, to be honest, if her landlord is keeping cows in the garden, she may as well move because her local council are going to be round there sharpish and the neighbours will be complaining about the mooing... Anyway. Yes. Ahem. Your reader will suspend their disbelief willingly, but do be consistent about your rules.

There's also quite a lot of humour mileage in transferring one set of established rules to a very different location. Think 'Coronation Street in space'. The denizens of a spaceship, searching for new life and new civilisations, but they have a corner shop, watch rubbish television and repeatedly try to put the cat out at night (who knew airlocks had catflaps?). Or, even a high octane police thriller set in a sleepy English village - which worked well for Hot Fuzz. This comes under juxtaposition of thingies...

5. Sex

Sex can be funny. It can be bloody ridiculous too, when you think about it. I bet amoeba don't worry about whether or not they've shaved their legs or put clean sheets on. But beware when writing humorous sex scenes, because sex is all about tension. Written sex, rather like the real thing, is about the build up to the climax and anything that interrupts that build up defuses the tension and reduces the sexiness. So if your couple are just about to get to That Bit, and the reader is on the edge of their seat waiting for the Bedroom Scene, it can reduce everything down to farce level if you introduce jokes or gags. Yes, there are funny noises during sex (ahem, or maybe that's just me), but if you put them into your sex scene, the reader will laugh, the tension will drop and you will have to work to build it back up again in order for the climax to be sexy rather than anticlimactic.

You can, of course, write 'funny sex', but it should be differentiated from 'sexy sex', You can't easily combine the two. You can also have your characters having funny discussions about sex, but when it comes down to the hot stuff, your reader really wants to concentrate on that, rather than heroes hopping around the bedroom trying to get their socks off or your heroine losing the 'fillet' from her padded bra. You want your reader to put down your book after the sex scene, fan themselves and have to go for a little walk in the cool air, not be smirking at your pages and thinking that your hero and heroine sound like two people who have never taken their clothes off before.

6

Tools to make things funnier

1. Increase the tension

The more you increase the tension before your punchline, the bigger the laugh. I once wrote a funny death scene in *Please Release Me* - I'm quite proud of it because I wrote a normal scene with a tiny dramatic irony based joke at the end, then I went back and rewrote it building up what the character imagined was going to happen, so that the contrast was greater. It still makes me giggle when I think about it. [*Please Release Me* is a dark book, but it has jokes in it. Funny isn't the opposite of serious].

Often having a longer gap between the set up and the punchline can also increase the tension. Take care not to make the gap so long that the reader has forgotten your set up by the time they get to the punchline, or it'll lose its ... punch.

Another thing that helps with increasing the tension is to put the most valuable piece of information at the end. This is the basis of all shaggy dog stories. The build up is such that the punchline, when you reach it, is hilarious (or makes you groan and then laugh). My favourite example of this is in Terry Pratchett's *Soul Music*, where there is a long, long scene about stealing a piano, based on *The Blues Brothers* scene, which ends with 'you can't stop us, we're on a mission from Glod'.

2. Exaggerate

If in doubt, exaggerate. If you're relying on a character's inappropriate response to make the scene funny, make the response over the top. If the comedy in your scene comes from the mismatch of characters, exaggerate the difference between them.

The characters in *Father Ted* all have exaggerated versions of smaller flaws. *The Office* has exaggerated characters. The satirical 'mockumentaries' *2012* and *W1A* have exaggerated versions of characters and exaggerated situations. These are everyday people and everyday situations taken to extremes. They make you laugh because they're so extreme. They make you cringe, because you can see how easily you could find yourself there.

3. Be specific

It's easier to picture something specific than something generic. Biscuit is generic. Hobnob is specific (and delicious). Dessert is generic. Organic raspberry fool is specific. By using specific descriptions, you narrow the mental image down to something … well, specific.

Victoria Wood was a genius at this. Study the Ballad of Barry and Freda. 'Smack me with a magazine' is funny in context. 'Beat me on the bottom with a *Woman's Weekly*' is hilarious because the word choice tells you a lot about the people involved. They're polite enough to use the word 'bottom' rather than 'bum' or 'arse'. They're middle class, maybe. They're the sort of people who have a subscription to *Woman's Weekly*. They aren't natural spankers (which is a sentence I never thought I'd write. Ever).

If you want a more classic example, read anything by PG Wodehouse.

Now, if you'll excuse me. There's a Hobnob that needs eating.

4. Dialogue

Dialogue is one of the greatest joys of the rom com. You can get characters to say things and riff off one another to great comic effect. You know how you walk away from an argument and three hours later, think of the perfect riposte … but it's too late to let it fly. Well, when you're writing a book, you can go back and put it in.

There is often the temptation to have long sections of dialogue where there characters are bantering, it's all very funny, but it's not moving the story forward. Resist the temptation. Resist. Have some banter, sure. But if you have more than three jokes in a row, think about moving onto to something that drives the plot, otherwise the humour will start to sound forced.

Of course, if you can make a joke that does both - makes the reader smile *and* drives the plot forward, then go for it. Well done you.

Always, always, always, remember to keep things in character.

5. Subvert expectations

There is a famous anecdote about Charlie Chaplin discussing a visual gag - you have a man, in a suit (because it's always funnier to see a man fall over, if he's wearing a suit), walking along the street and not paying attention to where he's going. Ahead of him, there's a banana peel on the floor and an open manhole cover. Which is funnier? Will he step on the banana peel? Or fall in the manhole?

Man. Banana peel. Hole in the ground.

He gets closer.

Which will it be?

Chaplin's solution: The man steps over the banana peel ... straight into the manhole.

Somehow this is funnier than either of the other options because you weren't expecting it.

6. Juxtaposition of thingies

If you need something to be funnier, look at what you're juxtaposing and make the contrasts bigger. This is basically a summary of all the advice above. Juxtapose better things. Exaggerate the differences.

A general tip with all of the above is, if you're trying to make a joke funnier, look at your punchline. Write the numbers 1 to 10 on a piece of paper. Now write more extreme versions of that punchline – more exaggerated, more specific, more surreal. Chances are, out of the ten possible versions, somewhere towards the end, will be perfect punchline.

7

Timing

Bear with me here.

> *Person 1: I say, I say, I say, what is the secret of good comedy?*
> *Person 2: I don't know, what is the secret of good co-*
> *Person 1: (Interrupting) Timing.*

Trust me, it's funny. And points out how essential timing is to the delivery of a good punch line.

Now, this is something to bear in mind when writing comedy in novel form (I mean novel as in book, not as in new. We hope that all the comedy you write is new, and you are not copying from *100 Best Jokes for 11 Year Olds*). Timing can be conveyed in several ways.

1. Visual Cues

Okay, let's get one thing straight. Exclamation marks are not funny, all right? I know they have their place! Of course they do! But using them to show that your character is exclaiming, is a bit like using capitals TO INDICATE SOMEONE IS SHOUTING AND THEN PUTTING 'he shouted'. Your words should do the work, don't expect your punctuation to do the heavy lifting here. As Terry Pratchett says 'Exclamation marks are like cats. Any more than two is a sign of insanity.' He meant two together, but it could work if he'd added 'on a page'.

However. Separating out a phrase, using speech marks, italics or parentheses (that's brackets, to you and me) can work very well to highlight a phrase that you intend to be taken in a humorous way.

Look at the way that works.

> *You make my "life" a living hell.*
> *You make my life a living* hell.
> *You make my life a (living) hell.*

All right, those aren't the funniest examples I could use, but you get my point? Different punctuation can highlight the words in a sentence that you want the reader to concentrate on. How about if I put:

> *'I'm so sorry, but I think my dog has just emptied his bladder on your "grass".'*
> *'I'm so sorry, but I think my dog has just emptied his bladder on your* grass.'

Depending on context of course, but these both mean different things. In the first example, the dog has clearly had a wee related accident on something that is passing for a lawn but obviously isn't. In the second, the dog has had a wee on something else previously, and has now just disgraced itself also on a lawn.

Parentheses don't work in conversation – you just try putting brackets around your words as you are talking – but you can use dashes to break up the speech like I just did there, did you see? Like this:

'I'm so sorry but – I think – my dog has just emptied his bladder on your grass.'

There is some doubt as to whether or not the dog has actually done something, but there seems to be a wet patch and an embarrassed beagle.

You can also use ellipses (a series of three, and only three, dots) to allude to a trailing off, either in speech or description, usually to cover up what ought to come next.

'I'm so sorry, but I think my dog has just ...'

Brackets do work in description though, to indicate an aside, something off the beaten track of the sentence and yet somehow part of it. Look at them as a field of cows alongside the footpath you are walking on. For example:

Great Scott (I had never met the man, but his greatness was generally assumed, and I liked to go along with the masses) what an enormous moustache the Colonel had!

46

2. Dialogue Tags

Writing 101 insists that the only dialogue tag you really need is 'he/she said' and that anything else is over-egging the pudding to an extent that your pudding is really an omelette. And that you only need to put in either 'he said' or 'Jack said' every few lines of speech, otherwise you end up with a whole page full of 'he said/she said', which is very distracting for the eye of the reader and largely unnecessary, because you end up with a book that feels more like a play script.

So, you can add some humour through the way you use your dialogue tags. Don't forget, that you can use them at the beginning of the speech, half way through or at the end. Try to mix them up a bit so you don't end up with the aforementioned play script.

Here's an example.

> *'You kicked him in the what?' Jack winced.*
> *'You know,' Sarah pointed.*
> *Jack said, 'but I didn't think he had one.'*
> *'You didn't...' Sarah stopped and coughed. 'What are you talking about?'*
> *'I'm not sure now,' Jack said, weakly. 'I was quite confident until you pointed at your handbag.'*

Beware, this above example contains way too many dialogue tags for safety. You should read whilst wearing a hard hat, and possibly asbestos gloves.

As an aside, there is a correct way to punctuate dialogue. If you use dialogue tags, like 'she said', they are part of the same sentence as the dialogue, so you use a comma. If you use action to separate different bits of dialogue, then the action is a separate sentence to the dialogue. For example:

"When you're using dialogue tags, the tag is part of the same sentence," she said. "Which is why you use a comma at the end."

"The other option is to use a full stop and convey who is speaking by showing what they're doing." She looked up. "Does that make sense?"

3. Action and Dialogue

The eye sees space as equalling time. Which all sounds a bit quantum, but, when you think of it, your brain is taking time to read the words, so it does work. Anyway. It goes like this …
Set up of joke
A body of text where your character is doing something or something else is happening.
Pay off of joke.
Like this:

'I love you for your kindness, your generosity, the way your hair grows and the way you look when you're lying in bed. I love everything about you.'
She fumbled for the kettle, the lead was wound around the toaster as usual and pulling it caused crumbs to spread

themselves evenly over the work surface, like fleas on a pale dog's stomach.

   'Of course, the fact that you're rich helps enormously.'

Compare the above to

'I love you for your kindness, your generosity, the way your hair grows and the way you look when you're lying in bed. I love everything about you. Of course, the fact that you're rich helps enormously.'

Can you see how the first example is funnier, for the pay off line being a little bit removed from the set up? Of course, the second example is funny too (of course it is, I wrote it!), but that the separation of set up and conclusion just enhances the humour. The brain is given the feed line and then tension ratchets up with the descriptive passage, before being given the reward of the final line. It also gives you the element of surprise (remember, surprise is a great deal of what makes you laugh), because you think the character has finished speaking, then they go on to finish their speech with an unexpected addition.

   Just remember to end with the punchline. Keep the funniest bit, the 'punch', until the end.

8

Writing the rom com - things to remember

Funny is great, but does it move the story along?

This is probably rule number one when writing romantic comedy – or pretty much any story. All the usual guidelines for plot and structure still apply in humorous fiction. A romantic comedy is, above all, a romance. All the story structure rules and all the genre rules still apply. There are a ton of books out there about three act story structure, so we won't bore you with it. If you desperately want our take on it, there's a bonus section on it in the back.

You've written a great scene. There are some brilliant one-liners in there and that bit where they fall, fully clothed into the bath is hilarious ... but does it move the story forward?

Each scene must fulfil at least two things – either move the plot along, introduce a new character, develop an existing character, introduce a new setting or foreshadow something that's going to happen later. If it doesn't do any of those things, but is just included to make up the comedy moments, then it's probably best left out. Don't throw it away though. Save the jokes for a different scene or even a different book. (Never throw away a good joke!)

1. The characters don't know they're in a comedy

In any story, the characters don't know they're in a book. To them, it's just real life. So try and make their interactions as life like as possible. If you watch people interacting with each other, you'll notice that a lot of these interactions between friends are naturally punctuated by teasing and joking. Interactions between strangers can be very funny when they're talking at cross purposes.

All jokes and funny scenes in your book must arise organically from the characters and the way they speak and act. The joke must fit the character. If a normally humourless characters suddenly cracks a silly joke, it's going to look weird. Unless of course, that joke shows the heroine that the guy she had assumed was humourless is human after all ... and quite attractive when he smiles ...

Your writer's eye will see a situation from a unique angle. If you're naturally predisposed to make jokes, then you'll see opportunities to be funny in most situations.

Having characters standing around laughing isn't funny for the reader. You want to make the reader laugh. Laughter is contagious, sure, but it's not contagious enough to move from your characters to your reader.

2. Don't be cruel

It's not funny to laugh at people because they are at a disadvantage. I'm not saying that a bad-guy character won't make fun of someone – that's fine, it's showing that the character is a total douche and that the reader can hate him. Just don't do it as the author. I know a good joke about dyslexia which makes my (dyslexic) brother laugh, but I wouldn't dream of making that joke to people I don't know because I don't know how they'll take it and I don't want to hurt their feelings. This links nicely to my next point.

3. Humour is subjective

Different people find different things funny. You know this. There are some jokes you tell in front of friends that you would never repeat in front of Granny. Not everyone will find what you've written side splitting. I know a woman who read an entire book of jokes, cover to cover, with a slightly puzzled expression on her face and didn't laugh once (I'm not entirely sure why she bothered...). It happens.

Different nations have slightly different senses of humour. There are things that they are culturally predisposed to find funny, based on the things that they have in common - language, cultural touchstones, shared history. Generally speaking, everyone finds physical comedy (slapstick) funny, but for jokes requiring prior knowledge about history or involving complex word play, your mileage may vary.

So what does that mean for you while you slave over your

book? Actually, it's quite liberating. Write what makes you laugh. If it makes you laugh, chances are it will make at least some of your readers laugh as well. If it doubt, show it to someone who has a similar sense of humour to you. If they don't find it funny, perhaps you should have a little rethink. And maybe get out a bit more.

4. Has what you pictured in your mind actually made it onto the page?

This is especially true of visual gags. That scene with the banana peel and the open manhole is hilarious in your head, but have you put the right details in the text? Just think of all those really bad joke-tellers that you know, who get half way through a convoluted joke and then have to stop and say 'oh, did I say that he had a donkey? Well, anyway, he's got this donkey in a field behind his mother-in-law's house ...Did I mention the mother-in-law?' It breaks the flow and the joke becomes nonsensical (it probably already was, I mean, who keeps their donkey in their mother-in-law's field? You keep them in the garden, obviously).

Another thing that's important with comedy is timing, especially if the joke is in the dialogue. You've written down what they said, but have you captured how they said it? The best way to check this is to get someone to read it out to you. They will read it as they would hear it. Does the joke still work? If not, rework it – change the words, move the speech attributions around, play with punctuation. Then get someone (best ask a different someone!) to read it out and see if it works any better.

5. Beware the in joke

In-jokes are great. People in the know love them. The trouble comes when people who don't have the background information read them and wonder what on earth you're talking about. I love *The Big Bang Theory*, which is full of science jokes. The writers on that show do a great job by planting the information you need to get the joke somewhere at the start of the episode. If they didn't do this, you'd have the science nerd portion of the audience falling around laughing while everyone else looks at each other blankly. One exception is when Amy Farrah-Fowler makes the 'Thriller adjacent to the amygdala' joke – but this is still funny because of Penny's WTF reaction. Okay, at this point, a number of people reading this will be wondering what on earth I'm talking about. Which rather proves my point.

So, beware the in-joke. If your editor asks you to remove a joke because they don't realise it's a joke – you know something's gone wrong.

6. Funny doesn't have to be fluffy

A lot of people think that comedy is the preserve of the light and airy. It can be, but it doesn't have to be stuck there. It is entirely possible to write a comedy (romantic or otherwise) which deals with dark themes. *A Fault in Our Stars* has funny moments and it's all about kids with cancer. You can't get much darker than kids with cancer.

Sometimes, it's good to have something light to relieve the

pressure. The moments of comedy serve as a contrast to the sadness. You can use this to heighten emotions, making the dark scenes feel darker, sadder, scarier. It's also good to use comedy to give the reader a break from time to time so that they don't end up feeling your book is too depressing for words. If you've written a particularly tense scene, the laugh at the end gives the reader a good place to breathe out again. Films like *Pulp Fiction* use this trick a lot, and it works.

Black humour isn't often found in romantic comedy, but if it works for your book, don't be afraid to use it.

In conclusion:

Read a lot. Write a lot. Submit.
   Keep at it and eventually you'll crack it.

The most important thing - **have fun**! If you don't enjoy writing comedy, it's going to be very hard to be funny.

9

Marketing a funny book

We are not experts at this. If we were, we would be much richer. All we have on this is wild speculation and half-baked theories created when we've been up too late milking the wine goat. If you're up for that, read on.

The romantic comedy market for the US and the UK are very different. The UK rom com is sometimes called 'chicklit' (bleagh - hate the word, but it's necessary). Chicklit (bleagh) is a specific sub section of the rom com. At one time it was popular to have clumsy heroines who were obsessed with shopping and shoes. This was fine in the more prosperous early 90s, but the mid 2010s is a much bleaker place and people who waste time and money obsessing about Manolos are no longer quite such sympathetic characters. Chicklit (bleagh) heroines have moved on, but unfortunately, the public perception of them has not.

Is there any advantage to being classed as chicklit (bleagh)? There is. To discuss it, we need to talk about the difference between UK romantic comedy and US.

Romance is a broad ranging genre. It embraces contemporary, historical, sci fi, romantic suspense and a great many other strands. UK romance novels also deal with a variety of other themes like family, job change, mental health, bereavement, divorce, addiction... any number of things. UK romances are stories where person meets person and they fall in love, but they (often) also contain major plots about what's going on in their lives. The books can be single POV - often written in the first person, or they can alternate between two POVs. UK romances can have closed door/ fade to black or open door sex scenes. Closed door is more common in the UK than in the US.

Romance in the US is more narrowly focused on the couple themselves. There's often (but not always) more sex, earlier in the book. Other peripheral issues are not often addressed. In general, a romantic comedy would have one POV (the heroine's), but dual POV narratives are becoming more common. Romances, even funny ones that deal with matters outside of the relationship are classed as women's fiction ... or sometimes chicklit (bleagh).

Neither of these are wrong, but they are different. So the reader's expectation from a romantic comedy is different depending on what they're used to.

So what do you do when you have a UK style rom com about a heroine who falls in love with someone, but whilst doing so, also deals with recovering from grief? It's about more than just the relationship ... but it's lighthearted and funny (yes, even with the grief stuff). In the UK, it's not a problem, you call it romantic comedy, stick a cartoony cover on it and Bjorn's your uncle. But in the US, you can't call it romantic comedy because it's about more than just the couple. You can call it women's fiction, but that doesn't signal that it's funny. Enter 'chicklit' (bleagh). It's not an Amazon category and not really a thing in the US, but the cartoony cover sure as hell conveys that it's funny and likely to deal with wider themes than just the relationship and be - possibly - a bit more British.

Now, whether these covers sell in the US is a different matter entirely. They do sell well in the UK.

Of course, if you're really lucky, you can have two editions - a UK one with an illustrated cover and a US one with a photographic cover. That would be a much better option. Do that. If you can.

The other really good thing about chicklit (bleagh)-style covers is that readers have come to associate them with romantic comedy. They like them. In the summer and at Christmas time they like to pick up a light hearted read that they know will leave them feeling uplifted and comforted by the end and a cartoony cover and a title in swirly writing is a pretty good bet for that.

For the record, some people will class anything written by a woman as chicklit (this time they actually mean 'bleagh'). Those people are WRONG. They're are never going to read your book, so don't bother with them. If you have to talk to them, talk to them about something else instead. Tropical fish, maybe.

10

Publishing pathways

Traditional publishing

This is where a publisher takes an exclusive licence from you and agrees to edit, publish and market your book in return for the taking a large share of any revenue earned from it. 'Exclusive' means that only they can publish the book in that territory. No one else can. Not even you.

This used to be the only model available, but not it is only one of the options.

We've both had many traditional publishing contracts. The royalty (your share of the revenue) that the publisher gives you is usually net of any production/distribution/ selling costs. So a paperback that retails for 7.99 will probably only make you a few pence per copy sold. If it's any consolation, it'll make the publisher only a few pence too (maybe a few more pence than you).

To give you an idea - for ebooks, a 99p ebook sold on Amazon will bring in 35p to the publisher. A 1.99 ebook on Amazon will bring in £1.39. So if, for example, your contract says you get 25% royalties then a 99p ebook will bring you about 8 or 9p per book sold. A £1.99 ebook will bring in about 34 or 35p per book sold, but it will sell fewer copies.

Although print books cost a lot more than ebooks, it costs a lot more to produce a print book, so the revenue per book sold is often very small. Also, most books sell fewer print copies in print. You can see why digital is everyone's favourite.

The publisher takes a larger cut from the revenue because they are taking a bigger risk, financially. They should pay for the editing, the cover design, the formatting, the printing (for print versions), the marketing etc. Unless they sell a load of copies, they won't make their money back.

Different publishers have different 'cultures' when it comes to how they interact with authors. Before you sign a contract, always talk to one or two authors who write for that publisher. Contact them privately (email, DM on Twitter etc) - most authors are happy to advise. Be professional in your approach. Do not repeat things told to you in confidence. Get more than one opinion.

If you have an agent, they will check the terms of the contract you sign with the publisher. They should also actively seek out suitable publishers and negotiate better terms (better royalty rate, narrower rights in the licence, bigger advance etc). If you don't have an agent, both the Society of Authors and the Alliance of Independent Authors have contract vetting services available for their members. This is worth the joining fee. Please get your contracts checked before you sign!

A lot of the larger publishers won't take submissions unless you go through an agent. A lot of smaller publishers will have certain 'open submissions' windows or twitter/Facebook pitch events (Keep an eye on hashtags like #CarinaPitch and #PitchCB).

Independent or 'indie' publishing

Indie publishing or 'self publishing' is new and thriving. In this case, you are effectively a small business that manages all of the steps in the publishing journey. You pay for the editing, the cover design, the formatting, the marketing up front in the hope that you will make your money back eventually. Because there is no middle man, all the net royalties (all retailers take a portion of the money!) will come to you. You can make more money per book sold. To give you an idea - for ebooks, a 99p ebook sold on Amazon will bring in 35p. A 1.99 ebook will bring in £1.39.

Self publishing is hard work. You have to market the book yourself and sometimes, that can be really difficult. On the other hand, if you like the sense of control … you get to control all aspects.

Vanity publishing

Vanity publishing is not the same as self publishing. This is when you pay a company to publish your book. They will publish your book, and be listed as the publisher. They are not obliged to market your book. Because you, the author, are paying the company, it is not a traditional publishing deal.

Because you are paying them on their terms, rather than yours, and they (not you) are listed as the publisher, it's not self publishing.

There are a lot of companies who offer vanity publishing, but dress it up as a traditional publishing deal. If at any point a publisher asks you to pay towards the production of your book, or their contract forces you to buy a certain amount of stock - be wary. Better still, run away.

Vanity publishing is a good option if you just want to see the book published and aren't worried about making any money from it. If, for example, you want to get a load of books made up to commemorate an event, then this might be an option.

There are companies who offer a full service for self publishers - so you buy their services, specifying what you want. The Alliance of Independent Authors has a list of such firms that have been vetted for reliability.

Once again, if you're thinking of signing a contract with one of these companies, ask around. Talk to authors who already work with them and see what their experience was like.

Hybrid publishing

You can do a combination of the above pathways. For example, you could have some books that are published by a traditional publisher and some that you independently publish yourself.

A lot of people do.

II

How to write romantic comedy - the novel writing part

We have both written a lot about how to write a novel over the years. The following section is basic advice on how to go from idea to plot to novel.

11

Starting your first novel

Oh hello. You're still here. (Quick, put the biscuits away. Tidy up). Ahem.

We promised you a bonus section at the back about story writing. These are compiled from a variety of articles we've both written for various magazines and blogs. We both do manuscript critiques and mentoring, so we've tried to address the questions that come up most often. You might find a few repeated examples, but hey, why let a perfectly good example go to waste? And sorry about the crumbs. You've caught us on a bad day.

1. Starting your novel - some words of advice

"Gosh", people sometimes say to me, often from a considerable distance because I have a look in my eye that suggests I might throw things at them if they come closer, "I'd really like to write a book!" Then they look at my ragged clothes and my unheated, damp house and add, "A successful one though." And then, cautiously, sometimes poking me with a stick, "Can you give me some advice?"

So I thought I'd use this opportunity to give that advice, without the poor souls having to come any closer to me. Can't really help with the 'successful' bit, but I can tell you about how to go about starting ...

1. Make sure you are writing for the right reasons. Don't think you will write a book because it's a good way of getting famous, making lots of money or easy. If you think it's a good, easy way of being famous and making lots of money, then writing a book is not for you. Why not try being a contestant on a game show? It will give you your desired effect with less humiliation than writing a book.

2. Make sure you have a Big Enough Idea. That interesting thing that happened to you once won't even fill a chapter, trust me. Your characters have to grow and change and develop over the course of a novel, and dropping an ice cream won't do that. Unless your character is the Incredible Hulk, of course, because I imagine dropping his ice cream would make the Hulk grow and change quite a lot.

3. Have a vague idea of which genre you are writing in and read up on those genres. For example, romance (my genre) has certain conventions. Like having a happy ending, where the couple get together. Now, you can break that convention, but it will mean your book will veer into become 'women's fiction', or worse, fall somewhere in between the two, and publishers may shake their heads and mutter, and, as a first time author,

you don't want to give a publisher the chance to shake their head and mutter. Know Your Genre.

Trust me, romance and the happy ending does not have to mean 'fluffy' books. But work with the conventions.

4. Write. And, whilst writing, ask yourself if everything you are putting in that book is necessary. Remember what I said about characters growing and changing (and possibly ripping their trousers, if they are the Hulk)? Well, every word must either move your story on or develop your characters. No lengthy discussions about dresses, please.

5. Finish it. Doesn't matter if you hate it by the time you get to the end, we all hate every word we've written once we get to the end. But the road to Writing a Novel is paved with unfinished first chapters, you need to stick with it and keep going. It will feel like pulling teeth and you will pray for death around about 50,000 words, but Keep Going. We will talk about making something readable out of what you've written, later. For now, just finish the damn book.

When you've written these words, you have my permission to go and eat a lot of chocolate. Or biscuits. Or cake … look, just go and eat everything you can see. It's fine. You're a writer now, it's what we do…

12

Characters

Building a hero

Do you have a constant procession of imaginary people walking through your life?

Annoying, isn't it? When you start to feel that they are better than your real friends (well, of course they are, they do everything they are told!), more amenable, probably richer and better looking too, unless your real friends are - I dunno - the Beckhams or something. Because imaginary people have to be like real people, only more so.

Now I'm here to talk about heroes in books, particularly in romantic fiction (because those are the books wot I write, and therefore I have a vague idea what goes into them).

The men can't just be normal men; ok most of the time, bit crap at helping with the housework, fairly clueless when you are upset but basically decent. No. They have to have hair of ebony, eyes like liquid chocolate, muscles that fill their clothes out and generally they smell of something luscious and exotic, like lemons and cold air. They are always empathic, touchy-feely, as full of hugs as a HobNob is full of crunch. They are, not to put too fine a point on it, sickening. If they have a flaw it will be one that makes them that little bit more attractive - they will be devoted to the memory of their dead wife, or single-minded in their pursuit of the life that they want (and the heroine).

If they have a physical flaw, like a scar or a missing limb, it will have been sustained rescuing orphans from a house fire, being caught in crossfire whilst serving in a military unit somewhere troubled or saving a puppy from a runaway vehicle. It won't, for example, have been sustained falling downstairs while catastrophically drunk. Because your average hero doesn't get drunk, unless he's drinking to forget his (equally picturesque) sorrows. He doesn't overdo it at a party, walk into a lamppost, sustaining a nasty cut to the forehead which scars in an unpleasantly puckered way, and then spend the rest of his night with his head down the toilet. No! For he is a Romance Hero...

When you come to Build Yourself a Man (can I recommend putting the eyeballs in last?) consider not just the muscles, they way his thighs bulge in his jeans, his sparkling eyes, the way he loves his mother, his dog and his job and how fabulous he is at everything he does. Consider, instead, making sure that he feels real to your reader. Even readers who are reading for the pure escapism and want their heroes to be billionaire sex-gods with biceps of iron, designer suits and an orphaned niece who needs bringing up, want a hint of believability in this man. They want to think that they just might run into him (or his poorer, slightly less muscly and dressed in Top Man younger brother) down their High Street on a Saturday night. They need a thread of believability running through their general Weave of Perfection.

Give him something he's bad at. Whilst a man being good at something is ineffably sexy, a man who isn't afraid to admit his imperfections is just as sexy. Show him making mistakes (and putting them right). Yes, he can be attractive, but he has to feel attainable.

Building a heroine

Not literally. I mean, Doctor Frankenstein has pretty much cornered that market and look how it turned out for him...

So. You need a heroine for your Rom Com and the likelihood is that your reading audience is female, so they are going to identify like mad with this woman. She's your 'placeholder' in the book (the person the reader puts themselves into in the story), so she's got to be someone your reader can like, sympathise with, shout at and, basically be for the duration of your story.

Who is this woman?

When I'm coming up with likely heroines to carry my books, I start out with something I call 'if this, then this'. It's just a way of making sure that your character is well-rounded and feels real. It goes a bit like this:

Heroine wears glasses.

That's just a throwaway description, right? Okay, so let's take it back a bit. She's painfully short sighted (which may give rise to some comedy situations later), so you've decided that she will wear glasses that she can lose at some opportune moment.

But. To your heroine (who doesn't, remember, know that she's in a book), wearing glasses is a very real part of her life. Short sightedness won't have just happened overnight, she probably wore glasses at school. Remember school? How if you didn't look exactly like whatever the image of perfection was when you were there (when I was at school it was Cleopatra, I'm that old) then you were bullied? The extent of the bullying depended generally on your friendship group and their resilience. So, the chances are, your heroine was bullied at school and called Speccy-Four-Eyes or similar.

How will that have affected her? Has it made her shy? Scared to meet new people? Or the converse, has it made her bolshy, noisy, the first person to point out her own imperfections and maybe make a joke about them? If she's shy, how does that affect her ability to talk to men (your hero)? If she's scared to meet new people, then how does your hero come into her orbit? If she's bolshy and noisy, does that put him off her at first? Does he see through her bluster and want to get to know her better or does he decide that she's a bit too much to take?

It doesn't have to be wearing glasses. Your heroine might be a willowy red-head with model-girl looks (she will have been called 'beanpole' and 'ginge' at school, of course), but maybe she has a limp from a tragic accident when she was younger. But that limp won't be purely cosmetic, not just something to detract from her otherwise flawless beauty – it will be something that stops her running upstairs to a ringing phone. Stops her walking miles across country when her car breaks down. She has to think about shoes in terms of practicality, not prettiness. It actually affects her life.

In other words, make your heroine a complete person. She's

more than the sum of her parts. And while we're on the subject of parts – please, please do not have your heroine think about herself in terms like 'I tossed my glossy blonde ringlets over my shoulder, slipped into the size eight jeans that made my legs look even longer and dusted just a touch of unnecessary make up over my flawless skin and sparkling green eyes'. All right, I may have slightly overdone this for emphasis, but it makes the point. Who thinks about themselves like this? If it's someone you know in real life, I suggest you get them help, because they are going to soliloquy themselves to death one day, in lonely physical perfection. In my experience, the only person to think of a woman like this, is a man. Maybe you are a man – I rule nothing out – but you are writing a woman that your readers want to be, remember, not to date or, as is more likely, dislike intensely. Keep her real. She doesn't have to be insecure about herself, but she's still unlikely to think about how wonderful she is, as in my example above. And, for the love of all that is holy, she will not, ever, at any time, think about how big her boobs are. Unless she's thinking that they are too big to fit into any nice clothes, or too small to properly fill a bikini. For most women, boobs are annoying, and almost always the wrong size. Men writing women, take note.

Okay, now you've got your heroine and she's nicely imperfect, but friendly and approachable to your reader. She doesn't have to be nice all the time, but if she's bitchy or unpleasant then make sure that you show exactly why she is that way. Your reader wants to either be her, or be her best friend, and anything that puts them off will distance them from your book (which is something you do not want).

Now, the point of a Romance is not only to get your hero and heroine together, but to watch them grow and change as people as a result of being together. So you need some form of character arc for your heroine. Remember, she must finish the book as a different person to the one who started the book (not literally, obviously, that would make it Science Fiction and there, I'm afraid, I am not qualified to comment). She needs to have sufficient background and motivation to learn more about herself and become a better person throughout your story. So, when you dream up your heroine, do make sure that you've got someone who's got enough backstory to make this possible. She doesn't have to be an orphaned street urchin from the slums of Birmingham struggling to overcome the death of her disabled brother at the hands of their depraved uncle who tried to sell them into sexual slavery, despite her disfiguring scars, to fund his life threatening Werthers Original addiction. That's an awful lot of backstory, and also possibly a Saga, rather than a Rom Com. Throw an extra generation in there and you've got ten books' worth of material. I'm not saying you can't deal with dark material in your heroine's past (I daren't, I've written disabled heroines and ones with tragically horrible pasts), but a little goes a long way. Plus your heroine has to believably overcome her past to forge a new, and happier, future with your hero, so. You know. Light hand with the abuse, and all that.

While I'm here, just a word about TSTL heroines. This stands for 'Too Stupid To Live' and is a common curse that strikes heroines in romances. Your heroine starts out as a strong, independent-minded woman with a career, her own home, and very nice shoes and ends up as a simpering mess, swooning on the manly chest of your hero, who is busy saving her from a life of debauchery and asking customers if they want fries with that. She makes stupid mistakes, or doesn't ask the right questions, simply because the story dictates it. She is the equivalent of the horror film character who doesn't turn on the lights when entering the spooky basement. Remember that meeting the hero should enhance your heroine's life, but it's not the be all and end all of it; she's a strong and independent-minded woman at the end of the book, and has only changed for the better as a result of our hero. Also remember to show us that she's strong and independent, not just tell us. There's nothing worse than being told how good a heroine is at her job, only to then have pages and pages of said heroine simpering girlily (yes, it is a word. Because I said so) and swooning and/or crying a lot.

She doesn't know she's in a book. If she does something daft, explain why she does it. Show her realising how daft it was. Show how she grows in experience or self-knowledge as a result.

Show how the hero enhances her life, rather than taking it over. And, incidentally, show her enhancing his life too. The reader should believe that this relationship is going to last beyond the last page of the book – it doesn't have to be Happy Ever After, but they should be able to believe that it is, at least, a Happy For Now. Your heroine ends the book in a better place than she was when it started, and has become a better person for knowing your hero. As they close the book after the last page, you want your reader to sigh and think 'what a lovely couple. I wish I knew them in real life,' not 'I give it six months before she's killed him with a pencil.'

13

Character Arcs

What is a character arc? And how do I get one?

People like to know about other people, that's why we watch soap operas and listen to gossip. Even news stories are more memorable if they have a human interest angle to them. All good stories are about people. The best stories involve people being changed by what happens to them.

The character arc is the description of what happens inside a character over the course of the story. The character's emotional journey, if you like. This is what stops your story from being a list of events and gives it a purpose.

Do you need an emotional arc to a story? If you're writing character driven fiction, then yes, it's essential. If you're writing action thrillers, then you might be able to get away without, but really, even then, having an inner journey still helps. *Jurassic Park* (the first movie, not the book) is an action film about rampaging dinosaurs, but the real story is Sam Neill's character learning to care about those two kids.

So how do you get a character arc? Character arcs are all about change. The most common and arguably the most satisfying sort is the positive change, where the character has a flaw or a misapprehension around which they have formed their world view and, through the story, this changes so that they are a happier person at the end. It is possible to go the other way, of course. *Breaking Bad* is a fabulous negative arc.

First of all, get to know your character. Figure out what their story problem is. Perhaps your hero tries to do everything himself because he doesn't trust other people not to let him down. Or has no self-confidence. Or needs to prove he can see a project to completion. Find what their emotional problem is. This is how they are at the start. Now work out where they need to be, emotionally, by the end of the story.

People are naturally resistant to change. No one switches from one state to another suddenly, so avoid having your character have a massive change of heart at the last minute. The character's journey from one state to the other has to happen in stages; several small changes that eventually add up to a major change in outlook by the end.

The trick is to get the external conflict (the big events that happen in the plot) to mirror the internal conflict (the emotional change). On the face of it, this sounds difficult to achieve, but it's really not that hard. Firstly, if you've done your homework and got to know your characters, you'll have a pretty good idea of how they will react to the major plot events. Even if your story is about a librarian fighting against invading Martians, every event will elicit a variety of emotional reactions in your Librarian. Focus on the reactions that are relevant to their emotional arc. Add some small reflection of their emotional state alongside the major plot points.

If you're the sort of person who writes into the mist without planning, don't worry. Just adjust the focus in the scenes when you come to edit the first draft.

Another approach is to use the emotional conflict to generate the smaller plot points. For instance, if we back to our example of the hero who needs to learn to trust others; He'll start of trying to do things by himself because other people would only let him down. At some point he'll have to trust someone with something small. They don't let him down. He's surprised – maybe there's hope for other people yet!

The next time he needs to trust someone, he's a little less reluctant. It works out again. He unbends a bit more. Then things go wrong (they always get worse before they get better) and someone lets him down. He thinks he was right all along. He can't trust other people. Other people are unreliable. Except, he knows that's not always true. Just before the end, he needs to take a leap of faith – which he takes because everything that's happened to him so far in the story has changed who he is. By the end of the book, he's got over the worst of his inability to trust people. He won't have flipped over to being totally trusting, but he'll be at least on his way there. Put in events to show all those points and suddenly your plot will start falling into place.

The better the internal and external conflicts mirror each other, the more satisfying the story is to read.

Not all of the characters in the book need to change, of course. In a lot of novels, the only person who really changes is the protagonist. Because I write romance, my books have emotional arcs from the two main characters. They must both change in order to be happy. Sometimes, a major secondary character will have an emotional arc too. Generally speaking, lesser characters can go through a book without changing significantly. If you find that one of your secondary characters is displaying a more interesting character arc than your protagonist, then perhaps it's time to consider that character as the lead in a later book.

So how do you know the character has changed? Well, they can stop and think about it – but that's not very believable. Far better to show the change through what they say and do. Was there are scene somewhere near the start that highlighted their problem? Write a scene towards the end that echoes the opening, but shows how different the character's responses are.

Working out your characters' internal struggles can really help pull a story together and makes for a more satisfying, emotionally resonant ending. Just beware characters suddenly becoming 'cured' of chronic illness or overcoming major psychological issues too quickly. Love is great, but it's not magic. You're allowed to mention therapy.

14

Conflict

Conflict is the thing that powers your story. Your protagonist has a problem, they are trying to fix it, but there are things in the way, so they can't solve their problem as easily as they'd hoped. So what are they going to do now? This tension, the knowledge that something has to change and wanting to know what happens next, is what keeps the reader turning the pages. The source of that tension is conflict.

On a large scale, conflict is caused by whatever it is the heroine wants and the thing that is getting in way of it. The bigger the barrier, the more interesting the conflict. In a romance, ideally the thing getting in the heroine's way and making her want to punch things should be somehow connected to the hero. This is external conflict. It frequently is plot related and comes from the outside to get in the way of the heroine's obvious story conflict.

You can (and should) also have conflict that is related to the heroine's story arc. There is something inside them that needs to change so that they can grow as a person and there's a false belief about themselves ('I can't do this' or 'I don't trust people' etc) that is getting in the way. This is internal conflict.

On a smaller scale, each scene needs conflict. Here the conflict is caused by the gap between the expected (simple) outcome and the actual outcome. The bigger the gap, the better the conflict.

Imagine you're chatting to a friend. You start telling them about how you had a problem with your phone line. The simple outcome would be that you got in touch with tech support, they fixed it. This is a pretty boring story. However, if you called tech support, they couldn't/wouldn't fix the problem, then you missed an important telephone call from the hospital, which means you missed an unexpected appointment to have some sort of pain relieving treatment and now you're doomed to be in pain for weeks until another slot opens up. And your phone still isn't fixed. So, you did X...and then Y... and then...

The second version is a much more interesting story. The gap between the simple outcome you'd hoped for and the hoops you had to jump through to achieve the outcome in reality is what makes the story worth listening to.

So, how do you achieve this in fiction? First, look at your protagonist's main problem. What do they have to do to solve it? Pick one of those things and work out what would happen to make that step more difficult.

You could use another character as antagonist - A lot of stories have a baddie who provides the obstacles. Hero wants X, Antagonist will do anything to stop him from getting it. Or better still, they compete to get to X first and antagonist lays traps for the hero. This is the main conflict in many an action movie.

It is possible to have nature as the antagonist. It could be nature at her most malevolent – which is the staple of disaster movies. Or it could be more subtle: A man is stranded on Mars. He needs to survive until the next mission lands and he intends to survive on the potatoes he grows in poo. There's a storm. His potatoes are destroyed, along with any hope of growing more. His chances are looking even worse now...

Add a ticking clock. The heroine must reach a certain goal before some terrible thing happens. This ticking clock could be anything from lightning striking a clock tower or the object of her affection getting married to the wrong person.

At the start of the story establish why it is important for the protagonist to achieve their goal, make it something that is important to them. Then, if possible, make the stakes even higher. In *Indiana Jones and the Temple of Doom*, Indy wants to get into the temple because he wants the sacred stones. He's a tomb raider and it's a challenge for him, but it's not life and death. Soon after his adventure begins, he meets the villagers who tell him that their children are being stolen and taken into the mountain and he says he'll help them. Suddenly the quest is more than about some nice artefacts. There are kids involved. And *then* ... his friends get caught up in it. Not only is it life and death ... it's now the life or death of people he cares about.

Individual scenes need conflict and tension too. Again, the conflict comes from the gap between expectation and what actually happens. If one of your scenes feels like it's not working (chances are, you'll know it's not working even if you don't know why), then look at the core point of the scene. Why is it there? What needs to happen in that scene to move the story along to the next beat? Work out what the protagonist of that scene wants and why they want it. Then figure out what's stopping them getting it until the end of the scene. This is often called 'goal, motivation, conflict'. A good scene will have all three embedded in it, so it will 'feel' right.

Conflict doesn't always have to be big, explosive stuff. It can be subtle. Set up the expectation and subvert it. It can be as subtle as someone you'd expect to stop and say hello looking awkward and crossing the street to avoid you. Or a wife neglecting to kiss her husband goodbye one morning. It just needs to be something that indicates that everything isn't as perfect as the protagonist would like.

These obstacles not only make it harder for the protagonist to reach their goal, they also give them the means to prove themselves. In order to keep going, they must find deep reserves of courage and perseverance. Avoid miraculous coincidences swooping in to their rescue and make then earn their story.

You need at least three points of great difficulty. Each challenge will be harder to overcome than the last until at the eve of overcoming the last challenge, the protagonist feels all is lost.

This ramping up to tension is reflected in the reader's feelings. They keep reading because they want to know what happens and because, if you've done your job, they are living through the protagonist's journey. When it all works out and the hero returns home triumphant, or the hero and heroine get to their happy ending, the reader can give a sigh and feel a sense of satisfaction. This endorphin rush (there is an actual reaction in the brain) is what makes the reader close the book and say 'that was good'. This is what you're aiming for.

15

Plot - three act story structure

Have a look at the books that have been bestsellers over the last few years – *Harry Potter, Gone Girl, Fifty Shades of Grey,* anything by James Patterson or Dan Brown. What do they all have in common? It's not genre or writing style. No, the thing that makes them stand out is that they all have a cracking story. The story is the thing that drives you to keep on reading long after you should have gone to sleep. What makes a book great is when it makes the reader care about what happens next.

You may be lucky enough to have a story that came to you fully formed with enough tension to keep people hooked from page one to the end. This rarely happens. For the rest of us, there's plot. If the story is a beautiful creature, plot is the skeleton that gives it shape.

The first thing to realise about story is that it's not the same as real life. It's less boring. Real life is a messy, haphazard collection of events. When you're telling a story, you only need to show the bits that are relevant to that story. There's a reason characters in books rarely go to the toilet or have to go buy cornflakes. Your novel has no place for the boring necessities of life (unless they are relevant to the story).

There are many, many models of story structure. If you want to look into it, I recommend *Story* by Robert McKee, *Save the Cat* by Blake Snyder (both aimed at screenwriters, but what they say is just as relevant to novelists) or *Plot and Structure* by James Scott Bell. Or indeed *'Novel writing for Dummies'*. (Links to all of these are on the resources list on my website).

They all say the same things, in slightly different ways. The old fashioned phrase for it is '3 act story structure'. Otherwise known as having a Beginning, a Middle and End.

We all know that stories need to have a beginning, a middle and an end. But what does that actually *mean*?

All novels are about change. The protagonist undergoes some sort of journey in the course of the book. This is the core of your story.

Get a piece of paper, on the left edge write down how things are for the main character at the start of the book. On the right edge, write down how things are at the end. What's changed? Your story is about the events that led to that change.

The beginning (Act 1) allows you to show the reader how things are at the start. It's where you establish character, setting and maybe the main conflict (E.g. there's a kid called Luke Skywalker, he's bored and craves adventure and there's a war against the empire that needs a hero). This section is usually quite short.

Human beings are naturally resistant to change, so something needs to happen to force the protagonist to change the status quo. (e.g. Luke Skywalker finds an SOS message). This starts the move into the middle (Act 2). There's an impetus to change, but the main character can still turn back and go back to the comfort of what was familiar. The next event pushes the character firmly over the threshold and then bricks up the door behind them. This point of no return commits the character to the journey. There is no turning back (Luke's Uncle and Aunt are killed and his home destroyed). You have now reached the middle.

The Middle is the biggest part of the story and often the hardest part of fill out. You know the start. You know the end. How the heck do you fill in all those words in between the two?

Okay, now go back to your piece of paper. Write down a few events that happen. Plot points, if you like. How do these plot points move the story along? Move the sequence of the events around so that they increase in difficulty the closer they get to the end. This will help give you rising tension as the story progresses. Look at the last challenge your protagonist has to face. Can you make it more difficult? What's the worst that can happen? Write that down.

Each event/plot point should push the protagonist to make changes that will take them further along their journey. What the actual events in the plot are will vary – it could be training to be a Jedi, or opening a bakery, or working out puzzles to find the arc of the covenant – it doesn't matter, so long as it's relevant to your story. Eventually, your protagonist will reach a point where they have to make a choice. They have to either commit to change or fail. Often, this is the point where things at their worst. The main character is brought so low that death (literal or metaphorical) hangs over them. In romance, we call it the 'black moment' or 'all is lost'. This is often the point where the physical plot and the emotional plot come together. In order to save themselves they have to embrace the change. Use the Force, take a leap of faith, learn to trust. The new, stronger protagonist can now punch their way out of whatever trouble they're in and propel the story on towards the end.

It is possible for the character to decide not to change. This works too, so long as there is a moment of decision. Whatever was wrong at the start of the story will still be wrong, but the main character returns to it with new understanding (or dies).

The end, like the beginning, is short. It allows you to tie up the loose threads of the story. It also allows you to ease the tension down from the crisis point so that the reader is left feeling satisfied by the end, rather than stressed. This works just as well for less upbeat stories - a good tragedy can be just as satisfying as a happy ending - but since we're writing romance, the happy ending is essential.

16

Show Don't Tell

Show, don't tell. Show, don't tell. You've heard this so many times, but how do you *do* that?

The best reading experience is when you're fully immersed in the world you're reading about. So, on one level, 'show don't tell' is about making the reader feel like they're actually there, in the scene. Show them what you want them to see, smell, taste and feel.

"The grass tickled her bare feet, slightly damp, still, but not cold. When she bent over to pick a daisy, the sun warmed her back."

As opposed to:

"It was a nice, spring day. She went for a walk on the grass."

You can also show what a character is feeling through their actions and dialogue. This is especially useful if you're trying to convey the reactions of a non-POV character (POV = Point of View). For example:

"Just let me explain," Sally said.

Bob put leaned back in his chair and crossed his arms. "Go

on then. I'm all ears."

Whilst the extract above doesn't say that Bob is sceptical about Sally's explanation, his actions show us that he is.

Showing can also be when you use subtle cues to suggest things about the type of person someone is. For example, say a character is going to find their painkillers:

She opened her medicine drawer and clawed through it until she found a half-empty pack of painkillers. Must get some more.

She opened her medicine drawer, where the medicine boxes were in alphabetical order. Hmm, half empty. She needed to put that on her shopping list.

Even though both the women above are performing the same action, you get the impression that they are very different sorts of people.

If you want an example of the masterful use of show don't tell in combination with specific detail, listen to The Ballad of Barry and Freda (better known as the 'Let's Do It' song) by Victoria Wood. The line 'beat me on the bottom with a *Women's Weekly*', quite apart from the beautiful alliteration, tells you so much about the character of Freda - she uses the word 'bottom' and reads *Women's Weekly*. You'd picture someone completely different if she'd said 'smack me on the arse with a *Horse and Hounds*'.

Woman in Manolos calls forth a different set of assumptions from a woman in cheap trainers. I tell myself this every day as I put on my cheap trainers.

It's always better to show what's going on when you can, but if you find yourself tying yourself in knots trying to show something and it's getting in the way of the story, then a bit of telling is fine. Reading a book that is all tell and no show can be really tiring. Whilst readers are clever and it's a good idea to get them to do some work (they like it, they like it!), it's best not to confuse them enough to pull them out of the story.

17

Point of View

Inextricably linked to character and 'show-don't-tell' is point of view. In the context of writing fiction, it helps to remember that the phrase 'point of view' has two meanings. One is the position from which things are being observed; the other is an attitude or way of considering matters.

The first of these is fairly obvious – whose eyes are you seeing the story through?

In a first person narrative (where the main character is 'I'), the reader is seeing the world through the eyes of a character, usually the protagonist. You can only see, hear, feel what they can. It's like one of those video games where you can look down and see your character's hands, but you have no idea what their face looks like. First person narratives are brilliant for getting deep into the feelings of the characters. It's very immediate and immersive. There's a reason most young adult novels are written in the first person.

The difficulty with a first person narrative is showing the reader things that are not directly said or done or felt by the main character. If, for example, your main character just told their mother some bad news. How do they know how their mother felt? They can infer from the fact that she gritted her teeth and threw a cushion at the cat that she's angry, but they can't actually know, because they (and therefore the reader) can't see inside their mother's head.

If you're writing in the first person, take extra care when the character describes themselves. If a character says "I flexed my well-honed pectorals" – you need to ask yourself what sort of person thinks of themselves like that. If your character is a shy gardener, he wouldn't think about his muscles – apart from if they hurt. If, on the other hand, the character is a gym-addict, then naming muscle groups and flexing them could come naturally.

Writing in the second person (where the main character is 'you') is uncomfortable to read for longer works, but can work well in short stories. Like the first person, it's immersive and visceral.

The third person narrative style (where the main character is 'he' or 'she') is very popular. You pick a character and follow them around. You can take the reader deep into the feelings and motivations of your characters. Or you can keep it slightly shallower. Personally, I prefer the deep third, but it doesn't suit everyone. A third person narrative gives you a bit more freedom with description than a first person narrative, but you still need to keep to things that your point of view character can actually see and feel. For example, if they're on the telephone, they can't see the person at the other end of the line nodding in agreement.

The omniscient point of view, where the narrator knows everyone's thoughts and feelings, is rarely used in modern fiction. The main difficulty with this is that reader does not stay with one character long enough to identify with them, which makes it harder to care about the characters. On the other hand, Virginia Woolf uses it masterfully in Mrs Dalloway. If you can write like Virginia Woolf, you don't need to be reading this book.

The other meaning of 'point of view' is to do with the way your character views the world. Your character's beliefs and mood will colour how they see things. Two different characters will view the same object differently. For example, if you're describing an old house – an imaginative child might see a spooky haunted mansion while their property developer father might see a fabulous investment. Even the same character could see the same things differently depending on their mood. A meal that a happy person would describe as delicious could taste like sawdust to the same person if they'd just had their heart broken. If you want a lovely illustration of this, watch *Despicable Me 2*, where Gru walks down the street twice – when he's happy, he joins in with the street musicians and plays with the kids, when he's sad, he glowers and stomps his way along.

When describing settings or even action, think about how your character is feeling. Allowing your character's mood to influence the description can help add depth and resonance to your writing.

While it's entirely possible to write the entire book from the point of view of only one character, there is no reason why you can't have more than one viewpoint in a story. In fact, using different point of view characters is a great way to increase the conflict – your reader can know why character X is doing something, while character Y has no idea.

Some writers like to keep entire chapters in one point of view, others will change narrators in successive scenes. There are no rules on how often to change point of view (or not), apart from making sure that you always take the reader with you when you make the transition. The reader should never have to go back and check whose head they're in. Changing point of view suddenly mid-scene should be done with care, or the reader may feel that the writer is 'head hopping'. Some readers (myself included) can't stand head hopping, while others barely notice it.

Point of view can be difficult to master, especially if you're writing in the third person, but getting it right will make your book a much more satisfying read.

18

Pacing

Pacing is about timing and tension. Generally speaking, your pacing will be fine at sentence and scene level, but in case it isn't, let's start small.

At sentence level, pacing is also about space on the page. People read from left to right. They associate distance between actions as the passage of time. For example:

> *Click. Boom.*

vs

> *Click. The sound echoed through the warehouse and Hero began to run. Boom.*

The second scenario has a bigger gap between the click and the boom. We know that because there was more space between the two words and there was time enough for the hero to take some action. Go back and read the section on timing for details on how to manipulate your words to vary timings.

In a scene level, something similar applies. In a fast paced scene, things happen with very little to fill the space between them. Sentences are short. Action follows action. Description is kept to the minimum necessary to convey the picture.

On the other hand, a slower scene will have more description, more room for introspection, more detail. The characters don't do quite as much in the time they have. But slower paced scenes are often where the character change happens. They give the reader a breather between action scenes (non-stop action is hard to sustain and exhausting to read) and allows the characters to reflect on what just happened and see how it changes them. It feeds the character arc.

Every scene should end with something that propels the reader forward into the next scene. With your plot point achieved, you close your scene with either a reminder of what was learned (especially if it was an erroneous assumption) or a line that highlights something that you want the reader to notice. This gives the scene a feeling of purpose and having these in each scene creates a sense of momentum for the book.

At an even larger level, the story must have a varied pace, but never become so slow that the reader starts to wonder where this is going. Every scene must have tension - a problem to be solved, a key step to move the story forward. If you have a scene that doesn't move the story forward, no matter how funny it is, it has to go (sorry). Never throw away a good joke though, save it for another time when you can reshape it to fit a new scene.

If all your scenes have tension and they are all relevant to the story, your pacing will take care of itself.

In general the pace of the story increases as the book progresses. The action points get closer and closer until the climax... after which the pace slows down, letting the reader down from the emotional high and giving them a few minutes to enjoy the endorphin hit they've just had, before you close the story off.

Since we're talking romance here, it's worth noting that a sex scene is an action scene. Stuff has to happen and it has to mean something to the character's emotional arc.

As with everything, write the story first and then go back and tighten anything that needs tightening. You will do a lot of this by instinct. If it works, don't mess with it. If it doesn't, then sit down and work out why.

19

Writing resonant endings

It took me the longest time to work out how to write an ending. I'm still not sure I've got the hang of it. I don't mean the end of the story, where everything works out and the major threads are tied up just so. I mean the actual last couple of paragraphs. The thing that makes the reader go 'aah'.

The trick to the denouement is to give the reader space to feel the endorphin rush, but to end the book before the rush fizzles out. There's research to suggest that people will remember the start and the end of things more than what happened in the middle. If you can get them to leave your book on a high, then they'll associate your writing with good things and probably rush off and buy another of your books so that they can experience it all again (we live in hope).

Resonance in physics is when one thing vibrating at a specific frequency makes something else oscillate at an even bigger amplitude. It's like a tiny note of tuning fork making a huge gong vibrate until it makes a louder tone. Or, how a musical note at exactly the right pitch can make a wine glass shake itself apart. Little notes that ripple out and connect to others can make something that is bigger than the sum of its parts.

For a reader, resonance and depth comes from connecting bits of the story together. You can do this with logic. So a character behaves the way they do, because of something that happened in the past. Readers are clever and they make connections from subtly dropped clues. A throwaway comment about how his father ran away to sea would link nicely with the protagonists hatred of boats, for example. You want the reader to think "so THAT's why he did that". This is also what gives the feeling of depth to characters. Know your character motivations.

When you've finished your first draft, have a read through and see if there are any links you can make between different sections. If the character is cooking a meal, see if you can use something they mentioned buying a few chapters before. Tying things together like this make the story feel organic. Everything has a reason for being there. As with everything, don't over do it though. Real life is rarely that tidy.

One easy way to create an ending that feels connected is to refer back to the beginning. Most romance films will end with an image that hints back to the the image they opened with, so that you can see the change that the characters went through.

Another good way to create a resonant ending is to refer back to something that was said during a memorable scene earlier in the story - a key bit of flirting early on, maybe, or a running gag. Why a memorable scene? Because otherwise the reader will have forgotten it! (Duh!)

In a rom com, it's always nice to end with a call back joke, especially if you can get a little twist onto it. For example, if you've seen *Dragnet* - throughout the film, detective Friday's love interest is referred to as 'the virgin Connie Swail'. In the closing scene he refers to her merely as 'Connie Swail'. His partner, and the audience, realise the significance of the words he left out and we're all very happy for them.

Having a call back joke as an ending makes the reader feel more connected with the characters because they are in on the joke and it gives a nice sense of closure.

Another option is for one of the characters to say something that is very typical of them. It doesn't have to be funny (although it helps if it is!), it just has to make the reader feel that it's exactly what they would have expected the character to say … because they now know the character so well.

20

Editing

How to Edit - Part I - Behold the thing you have created

So, you've finished writing your novel! Well done! You should now have in front of you, a file of around 75,000 consecutive words! Some of them make sense! Some of them may even be good words like 'susurration' and 'castigate', two words of which I am particularly fond but find little excuse to drop into conversation. And I am sure you think that these 75,000(ish) words are ready to go out in public, where they will undoubtedly draw the praise of many, the attention of a few, and possibly the finances of a publisher.

But hold your horses there. It is, and I hate to tell you this, extremely unlikely that your book is ready to be seen unescorted and out alone yet. It, like a three year old, may appear to be perfectly functional in all ways, but is still incapable of crossing a road or whipping up a cheese souffle. In fact, you may discover that it isn't even a proper book, but we can sort that out in the edits.

Firstly - put it away. Honestly. Somewhere you can't see it or smell it. A locked box in the bottom of a filing cabinet in a disused lavatory (you can put a sign on the door saying 'Beware of the Leopard' if it makes you feel more comfortable). At least six weeks should do it.

If you understand this reference, you are My Kind of People

But as long as you can bear it. Whilst it is marinating in there, write something new. Or go on a long holiday - anything that distracts you.

When a decent length of time has passed, withdraw the book and sit down with a big red pen (or highlights open on your computer) a bar of chocolate and the curtains drawn. *Do not* tell people what you are doing. They will Ask Questions, which is very off-putting. Now read through your book again, and make notes as you go (hint, if you want to know how bad things really are, do a word search through your manuscript for little modifiers like 'just' . Once you've passed the 200 mark you can scream if you want). Remember what I said about your characters having to grow and change? And every word moving the action on or developing the characters? Be honest now, can you really say that they do? Do you have four page descriptions of locations (or, even worse, clothes)?

And then, sit back, and think 'why should the reader care about this?'

Now, eat the chocolate. You can despair a bit, if you like, it's natural. You are also allowed to think you've written the worst book ever in the history of books, and that's including that four page illustrated 'Store of The Heghog' you wrote when you were seven.

('A captivating tale of nature' - your mum)

But, admit it. There's a few sentences in there, a few descriptions, where you think 'that wasn't too bad'. Maybe the characters are wooden and don't behave like real people but there's this bit where they ... and that's not too terrible. Maybe the storyline still strikes you as unique. There's... just... something ...

Now, quick. Make notes. Capture those 'somethings' that stood out for you. Circle them if you have to. Scribble all over your page (it's easier if you've printed it out for this bit, we've all ruined lots of laptops doing this). You will end up with things like 'why did she say this here? Why not earlier?' and 'where's the caravan gone?' and, if your handwriting is like mine 'habble flib con not won argon'. Which you can decipher later.

What you will end up with is lots of coloured circles, Post It notes stuck on, chocolate stains, scribble, tear-stains, turned down corners, mysterious other stains and a notebook where you have, hopefully, written ideas. Oh, and lots of chocolate wrappers.

But the main things is - you've got something to work with.

How to Edit - Part II - chop, chop, arrgh

You are now at the 'chop chop arrgh' stage

All right, calm down. Deep breaths. Now. You've written your novel and you've followed our instructions and you are now staring at pages and pages of scribbled on manuscript, convinced that this is the worst idea you've had since you bought that outboard motor and strapped it to the swimming aids in the local pool.

To be honest, that was *not* your finest hour

So now what do you do?

Sit down, have a large cup of tea and a packet of HobNobs (other biscuits are available), and a think. Do you have one of those Kindles that reads to you? Doesn't matter if not, you can do this with your own voice. If you have got a fancy Kindle, save your manuscript to it and get it to read it aloud to you. If you haven't, then you're going to have to do the DIY version, and read it aloud to yourself. As you go, make notes, and bear in mind that *every single word* has to earn its place. Remember what I said about huge long descriptions? And lots of words about things that are never going to appear in the book again? I don't want to have to come round and slap your hands …

Notes. Lots of notes.

This is what organised writers do. Apparently.

This is the time to move scenes and people around if they don't work where they are. Or kill them, killing them is good - not necessarily really killing them, unless it's that kind of book, but if they don't seem to work, or they appear on the page, say something vital and then go off never to be heard of again - try to think of a different way that information can be got over. Merge two people into one (don't try this in real life, they don't like it). Make your characters real. Just take out the boring bits of real life, nobody wants to read about cups of tea, walking the dog, cleaning the toilet … if your characters must do these things then at least have them talking about things relevant to the plot while they are doing them.

And I cannot stress this enough … every single word you write must advance the plot or deepen the characters. I know you've done lots of research into tree felling, but the readers don't care. They don't need to know how you fell an oak, they just want the characters to do it and move on to the next thing.

Yes, it's complicated. Yes it takes work. But your readers want 'chop chop arrrgh' not a lecture

In fact you need to get your book distilled down to the 'chop, chop, argggh' stage. Cut out all that flabby prosey stuff, where you describe the night sky for four pages. Readers know what a sky looks like, they want to know what is going to fall out of it. And, as you cut stuff out, you are going to be thinking 'chop, chop … arrrgh, I love that bit, surely I can leave that in?!' Just think about how important it is to the plot …

Editing Part III - What's missing?

Sometimes, if you write 'short' - in my case, loads of dialogue with not enough context - then you'll be doing more tapping things in, rather than chopping. My first drafts are always 10 to 20K shorter than they need to be. I tend to have to go in add details to the description, so that the characters aren't just floating around in white space, chatting.

If you're a pantser, you might need another look at the three act structure to make sure you've got the beginning, the middle and end in roughly the right place and that the scenes move in a logical sequence. Action A in scene 2 leads to consequence B in scene 3 (or later), if you see what I mean. If they don't, you'll have to switch chunks around, even move whole scenes.

This is also a good time to see if there are any recurring motifs or subtle themes within your story. Plot is the sequence of events. Theme is the core idea that gives that sequence meaning. It's what the book is actually about. When you spot themes, see if you can go back and enter a sentence here or change a word choice there to reflect the theme. If there's a recurring motif, see if you can use it elsewhere.

You should not be 'padding' your story with unnecessary stuff. You should only be adding what is needed for the reader to get a full flavour story.

It can be hard to see what's not there... because it's not there. This is a good reason to have someone else look at your manuscript. But only do this once you've checked it for story and common sense and all that good stuff first. If you're getting feedback, you're better off using someone who has some professional involvement with the publishing industry like a freelance editor. A lot of published authors do structural and content editing work and if things work out, you might find a great mentor or even a great friend from it. We both highly recommend the Romantic Novelists Association's New Writer's Scheme (for those aiming at the UK market). You get to talk to a lot of published romance authors and one of them will read your manuscript *in full* and give you feedback and market advice. Many of your favourite romance writers will be graduates of the NWS.

Alternatively, of course, you could just get in touch with one of us. We both offer manuscript critiques and one-to-one mentoring.

THE END

Did you enjoy this book? If you did, please leave a review. We'd be ever so grateful. We'll eat a celebratory Hobnob for each review.

If you have questions or comments or just fancy a chat, get

in touch. We're usually around on Twitter - @janelovering and @rhodabaxter.

If we made you laugh, you might enjoy one of our novels.

Want to try before you buy? You can get a free Christmas novella by visiting Rhoda's website - www.rhodabaxter.com.

21

Resources and recommended reading

Resources

Other books on writing that you might find useful

If you can't be bothered to Google these, links to all these books are available at https://rhodabaxter.com/resources-for-writers/romance-writers-toolkit/

How Not To Write A Novel - Howard Mittelmark and Sandra Newman

On Writing by Stephen King

Love Writing by Sue Moorcroft

Take Off Your Pants by Libby Hawker (I bought it because of the title. I found it really useful. Please note, it will not teach you how to take off undergarments. I had to learn that through trial and error.)

Into the Woods by John Yorke

Story by Robert McKee

Save the Cat by Blake Snyder (both this and Story are aimed at screenwriters, but what they say is just as relevant to novelists)

Plot and Structure by James Scott Bell.

Novel writing for Dummies

Understanding Comics and *Making Comics* by Scott McCloud – ideal if you're the sort of person who is more visually orientated. You don't have to be a comic book fan to appreciate it

Marketing the Romance by Liam Livings – a clearly written book about marketing from someone who is a marketing professional and a novelist

Pitch Power by Kate Harrison – a guide to pitching your book. Useful when you're ready to send your book out to agents and publishers

Books about laughter and jokes that you might enjoy

The Naked Jape by Jimmy Carr and Lucy Greeves (this one has jokes in it)

Laughter by Robert Provine (this one's quite academic, but interesting)

The Viz book of Crap Jokes - Viz

Useful websites

Links to all of these sites and a few useful books are available at https://rhodabaxter.com/resources-for-writers/romance-writers-toolkit/

The Romantic Novelists Association - the best place to find out about romance writing (UK based). If you're unpublished, you can also join the New Writers Scheme, which is one of the best mentoring schemes around. If you want direct mentoring - we both do one-to-one mentoring too. Just ask! [https://romantic novelistsassociation.org/]

The Alliance of Independent Authors - Excellent curated resources on self publishing options. They offer free contract advice if you're a member. If you're traditionally published, it's still a good idea to check out their blog for marketing ideas.

[https://www.allianceindependentauthors.org/]

The Society of Authors - Essentially an author's union. They offer free contract advice if you're a member (you can join when you are offered the contract, before you sign it). They have great resources about author's grants and advice about things like tax [https://www.societyofauthors.org/].

Dictionary.com [https://www.dictionary.com/] and Theasaurus.com [https://www.thesaurus.com/]- these are self-explanatory. They are an online dictionary and thesaurus.

TV Tropes - this is a great place to find out about tropes. It's useful to know whether you're writing a trope (chances are, you are, even if you don't know it) and how you could change things up a bit. [https://tvtropes.org/]

They fight crime - Very silly site that suggests unusual crime fighting duos. Included here only because I love wasting time there. Sometimes their suggestions can spark an idea (not the idea they suggested, because those are bonkers). For example
 "He's a leather-clad shark-wrestling firefighter on a mission from God. She's a provocative mutant advertising executive descended from a line of powerful witches. They fight crime!" [https://www.theyfightcrime.org/]

Acknowledgements

This book started out at the RNA Conference 2014, when we gave a talk called 'Writing Funny – from dialogue to situation'. Jane dressed as a penguin and we got a bit worried that one of the audience might actually do themselves an injury from laughing when we talked about 'pink parts' in the writing sex section. The feedback from this talk was so great that we collected up all the questions we got and answered them in a follow up talk a couple of years later, getting into the weeds of comedy theory and 'how to write funny'. People still come and talk to us about those talks.

Someone suggested we should write it all up as a book. We looked at all the emails we had from planning the talks and thought 'why the hell not?'. So, here you have it. The book of the talks. All that's missing is the penguin onesie.

There are lots of people to thank. We raise a Hobnob to our families, obviously, for putting up with us... they have to, I guess, but it's still nice of them; to Kate Johnson, Vienna Johnson, Kathryn Kendall, Liam Livings, Alison May and Mark Stay for reading early copies and giving us quotes (and feedback) that we can use. Thanks to the RNA for being such a supportive organisation. Thanks always to the Naughty Kitchen for encouraging us to embark on this crazy side project and for all the discussions we've had whilst milking the wine goat.

And of course we'd like to thank each other. 'Cause we're

nice like that.
   Cheers!
   Jane and Rhoda

About the authors

Other Books by Jane Lovering

A Cottage Full of Secrets
A Midwinter Match
Home on a Yorkshire Farm
A Country Escape
A Seagull Summer
Christmas Secrets By The Sea
Christmas at the Little Village School
The Boys of Christmas
The Art of Christmas
Can't Buy Me Love
The Little Teashop of Horrors
I Don't Want to Talk About it
Please Don't Stop the Music
Hubble Bubble
Starstruck
How I Wonder What You Are
Living in the Past
Falling Apart
Vampire State of Mind

Other books by Rhoda Baxter

Snowed In
  Belonging
  Christmas for Commitmentphobes
  That Holiday In France
  Girl On The Run
  Girl Having a Ball
  Girl On In Trouble
  Girl at Christmas
  Please Release Me
  Doctor January

Written as Jeevani Charika
  Playing For Love
  A Convenient Marriage
  This Stolen Life
  Christmas At The Palace

About Jane Lovering

WINNER - ROMANTIC NOVEL OF THE YEAR 2012 with *Please Don't Stop the Music*, RoNA ROSE (NOVELLA OF THE YEAR) 2018 with *Christmas at the Little Village School* AND FANTASY ROMANTIC NOVEL OF THE YEAR 2019 with *Living in the Past*

Jane was, presumably, born, although everyone concerned denies all knowledge. However there is evidence that her early years were spent in Devon (she can still talk like a pirate under the right conditions) and of her subsequent removal to

Yorkshire under a sack and sedation.

She now lives in North Yorkshire, where she writes romantic comedies and labours under the tragic misapprehension that Johnny Depp is coming for her any day now. Owing to a terrible outbreak of insanity she is now the minder of three cats and an insane terrier - just as the five kids showed signs of leaving home, and she has to spend considerable amounts of time in a darkened room as a result (of the animals, not the kids leaving home).

Jane's likes include marshmallows, the smell of cucumbers and the understairs cupboard, words beginning with B, and Doctor Who. She writes with her laptop balanced on her knees whilst lying on her bed, and her children have been brought up to believe that real food has a high carbon content. And a kind of amorphous shape.

Not unlike Jane herself, come to think of it.

She had some hobbies once, but she can't remember what they were. Ask her to show you how many marshmallows she can fit in her mouth at once, though, that might give you a clue. Go on, I dare you.

You can find out more about Jane (should you wish to, of course) from her blog and website at http://www.janelovering.co.uk

About Rhoda Baxter

Rhoda writes contemporary romances about smart women and the men who love them - no alpha males here, thanks. She especially likes it when they make her laugh. She is fond of cake, British comedy and Lego Stormtroopers.

Once upon a time, she used to be a microbiologist, which might give you a clue about where her name came from.

She is British-Sri Lankan and she sometimes writes multicultural fiction under the name Jeevani Charika. She finds being two people really confusing.

Rhoda is a member of the UK Romantic Novelists' Association and the Society of Authors. Her books have been shortlisted for the RoNA awards (2017 and 2020), the Love Stories awards (2015) and the Joan Hessayon award (2013).

Rhoda is an excellent procrastinator, so you can find her wittering on about science, cake and comedy on Twitter (@rhodabaxter), when she's meant to be writing. If you fancy a free novella, you can find out how to get that on her website www.rhodabaxter.com.

This is the last page.

Have you left a review? Please leave a review.
We need another excuse to eat a Hobnob.

Thank you.

9 781913 752002